THE STRESS-LESS COLORING BOOK
FOR ALL AGES

VOLUME 2

The best therapeutic and relaxation tool to put you and your loved ones in the great mood!

CREATED BY
Dr. DIANNA M. and GABRIELLA K.

The Mother and Daughter Team

Copyright © 2018 by Dr. Dianna M. and Gabriella K.

All rights reserved. No part of this publication may be reproduced, distributed, or transmitted in any form or by any means, including photocopying, recording, or other electronic or mechanical methods, without the prior written permission of the publisher, except in the case of brief quotations embodied in critical reviews and specific other **noncommercial** uses permitted by copyright law.

All materials & writings are copyright © Dr. Dianna M./Gabriella K., except for quotes and other specifically identified content that belong to their respective copyright holders if applicable.

Suggestions and strategies in this Guide may not be suitable for all situations. You should consult with professionals when appropriate. Neither the author nor the publisher can be held responsible for any loss, claim or damage arising out of the use, or misuse, of the suggestions made, the failure to take medical advice. Neither the author nor the publisher can be held responsible for any material from third party websites.

On top of our current monthly donations, a percentage of sales from ALL of our books will support children with mental and other health issues, some YouTube channels, and animal shelters which are helping abused and homeless animals.

Printed in the United States of America

First Printing, 2018

ISBN 978-1-7322971-8-0

Stress-Less Way Publishing

Connect with us:

Email: team@stresslessway.com

www.stresslessway.com

WELCOME!

The Mother and Daughter team would like You to join us on the **"Color Your Stress Away"** Journey!!!

Presented for your attention is a series of **The Coloring Books for ALL Ages**. They will help you and your loved ones to facilitate inner peace, reduce daily stress and lead to a more productive life. You will get hours of therapeutic relaxation.

Unwind, take time to be still, and rejuvenate your mind and soul.

This Series of our **unique coloring books** includes incredibly inspiring quotes and drawings from **ACTUAL** children and adults, some of whom have very challenging health issues.

The way this book is organized, you can cut out the finished coloring pages and frame them for yourself or the people you love!

Only together, by using a variety of the stress reduction techniques, can we build a safer environment for us, our children, and future generations to come.

ENJOY OUR OTHER POPULAR SERIES:

- THE STRESS-LESS LIFE GUIDE - TEENS.
- THE STRESS-LESS LIFE GUIDE - SUMMERTIME OR ANYTIME - TEENS.
- THE STRESS-LESS LIFE GUIDE - KIDS AND PARENTS.
- THE STRESS-LESS LIFE GUIDE - SUMMERTIME OR ANYTIME - KIDS AND PARENTS.
- THE STRESS-LESS LIFE GUIDE - ADULTS.

FOREWORD

Hello fellow readers! It is a privilege to introduce you to the world of incredible series of The Stress-Less Coloring Books. My name is Dr. Anton Fisher, D.O. I am a licensed and Board Certified Psychiatrist. I was asked to review the contents of these books. Having done so, I wholeheartedly recommend them to readers of all ages.

Stress, which is Anxiety by another name, has always been difficult to treat. There are various known forms of psychotherapy recommended for stress, and they often involve coloring and journaling. Completing the pages in the books will be an outlet for your negative emotions and help to deflate your stressors from your day. The coloring can be completed on your own or with family and friends.

This series of Stress-Less Coloring Books will introduce you to some of those rare books that can be a benefit to everyone. I am confident to say that regular practicing in these books will lead to a reduction in anxiety/stress levels and improved functioning at work, school, home, and life in general.

Dr. Anton Fisher, D.O.

Dr. Anton Fisher, D.O. is a Board Certified Psychiatrist practicing in multiple states, including Nevada. He is the founder of **TeleMind™**, a novel telepsychiatry clinic located in the Las Vegas Valley and beyond. More information can be found at www.telemindclinic.com.

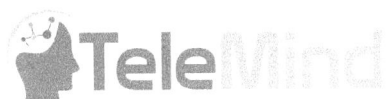

*Disclaimer: I do not have a financial interest in these books. These books are not a substitute for medical advice. If you believe you are experiencing symptoms of a mood, anxiety, attention or other disorder, please consult with a mental health professional. I waive any liability for the content or effects of these books.

LET THE FUN BEGIN...

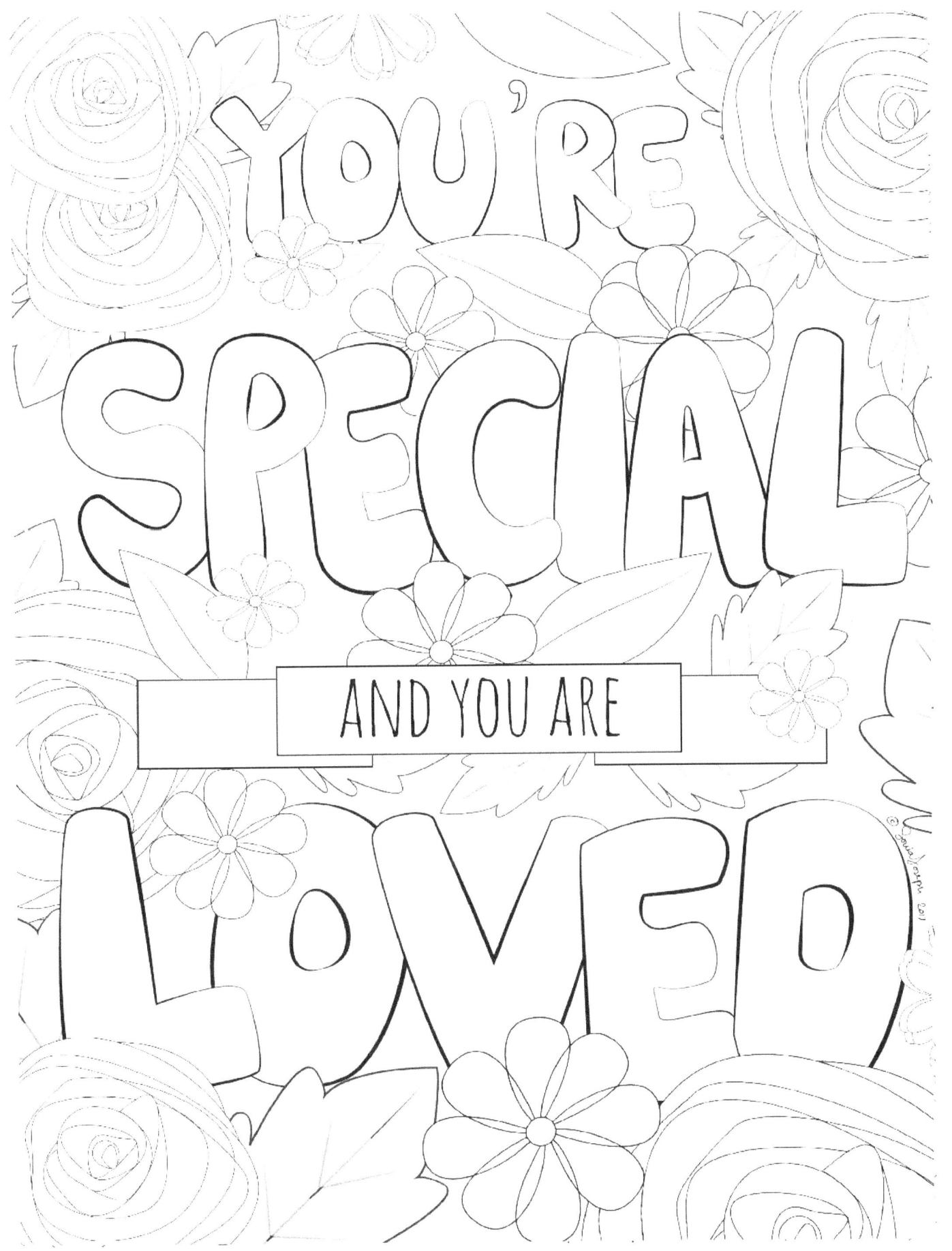

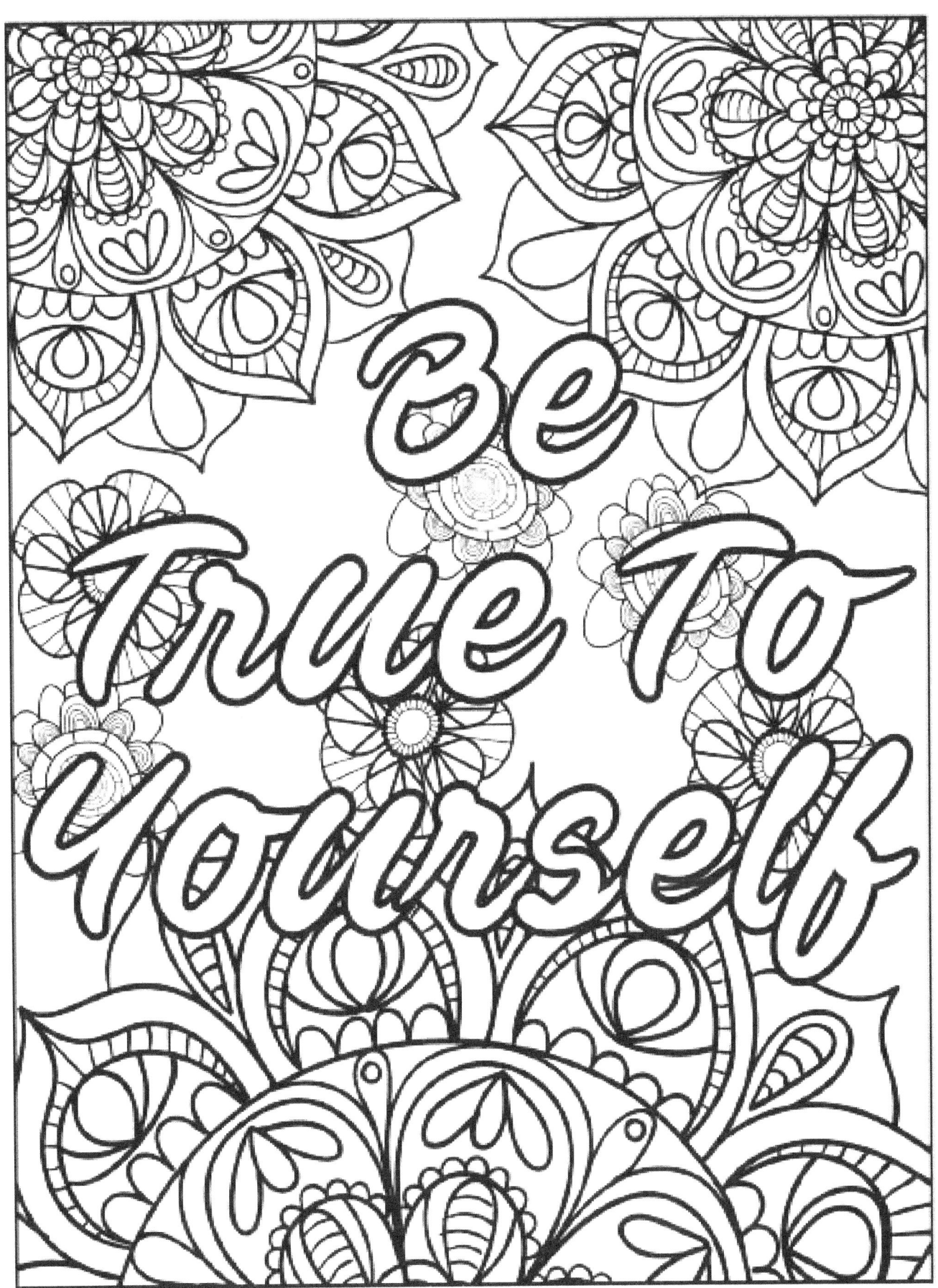

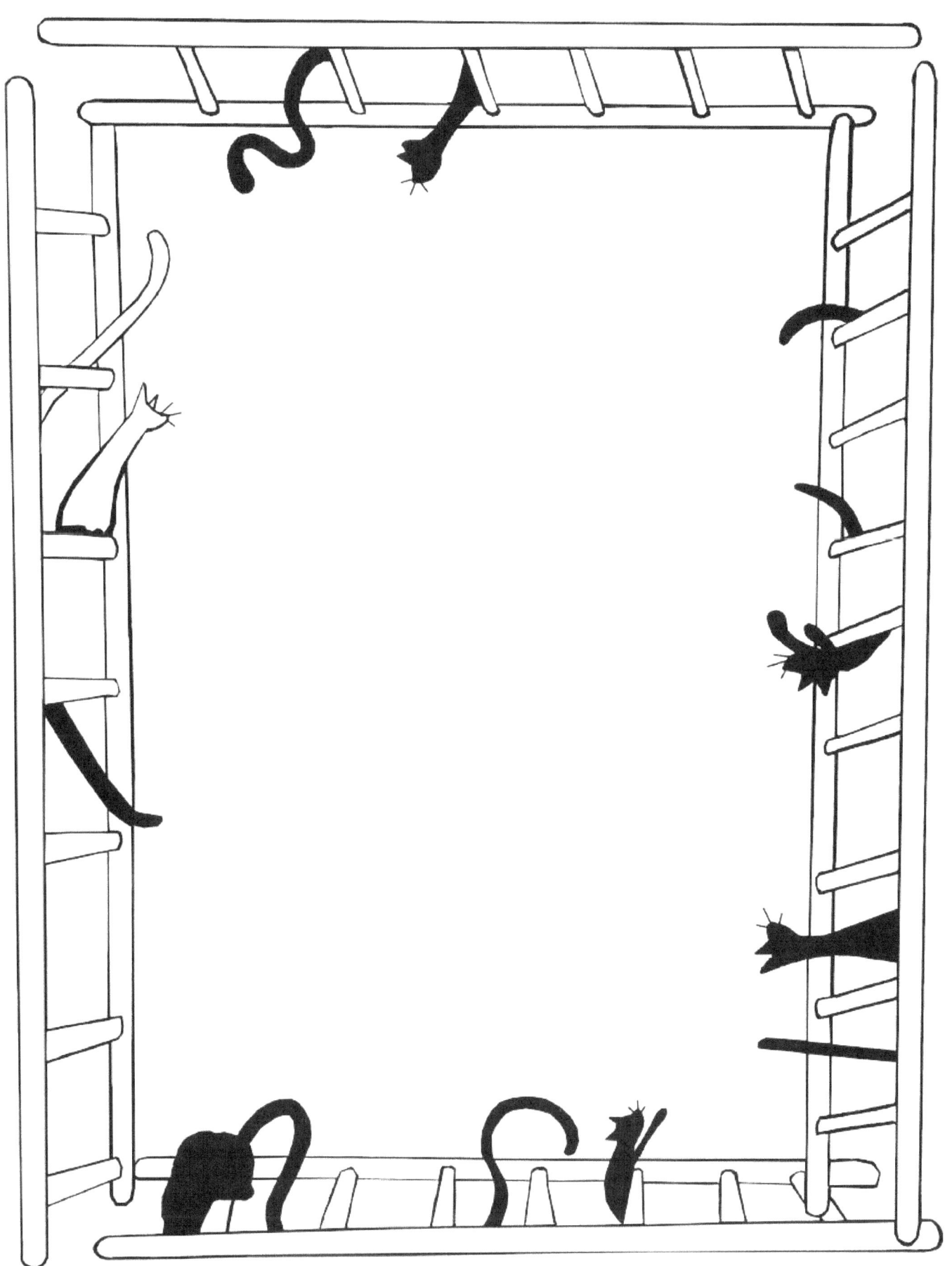

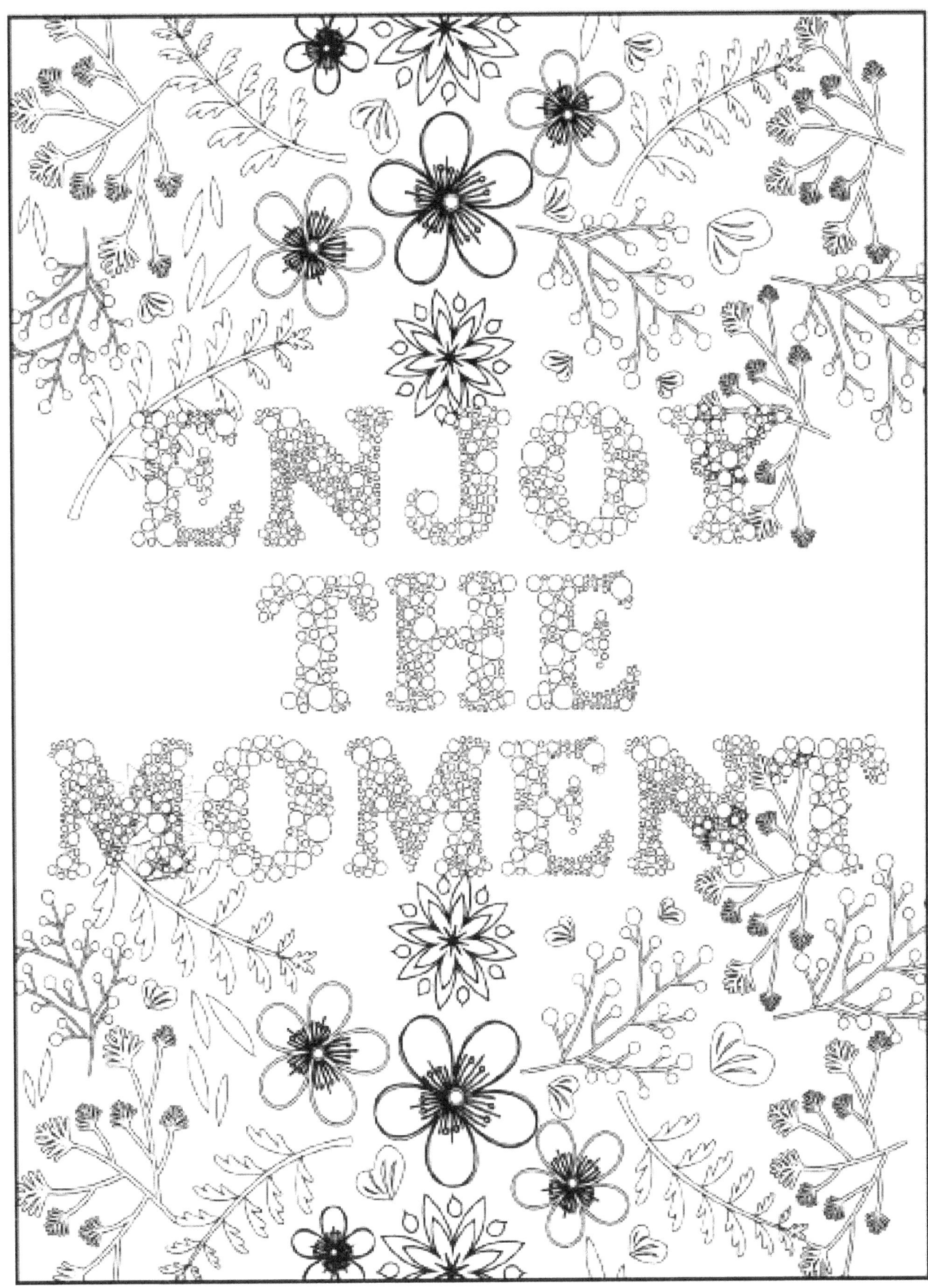

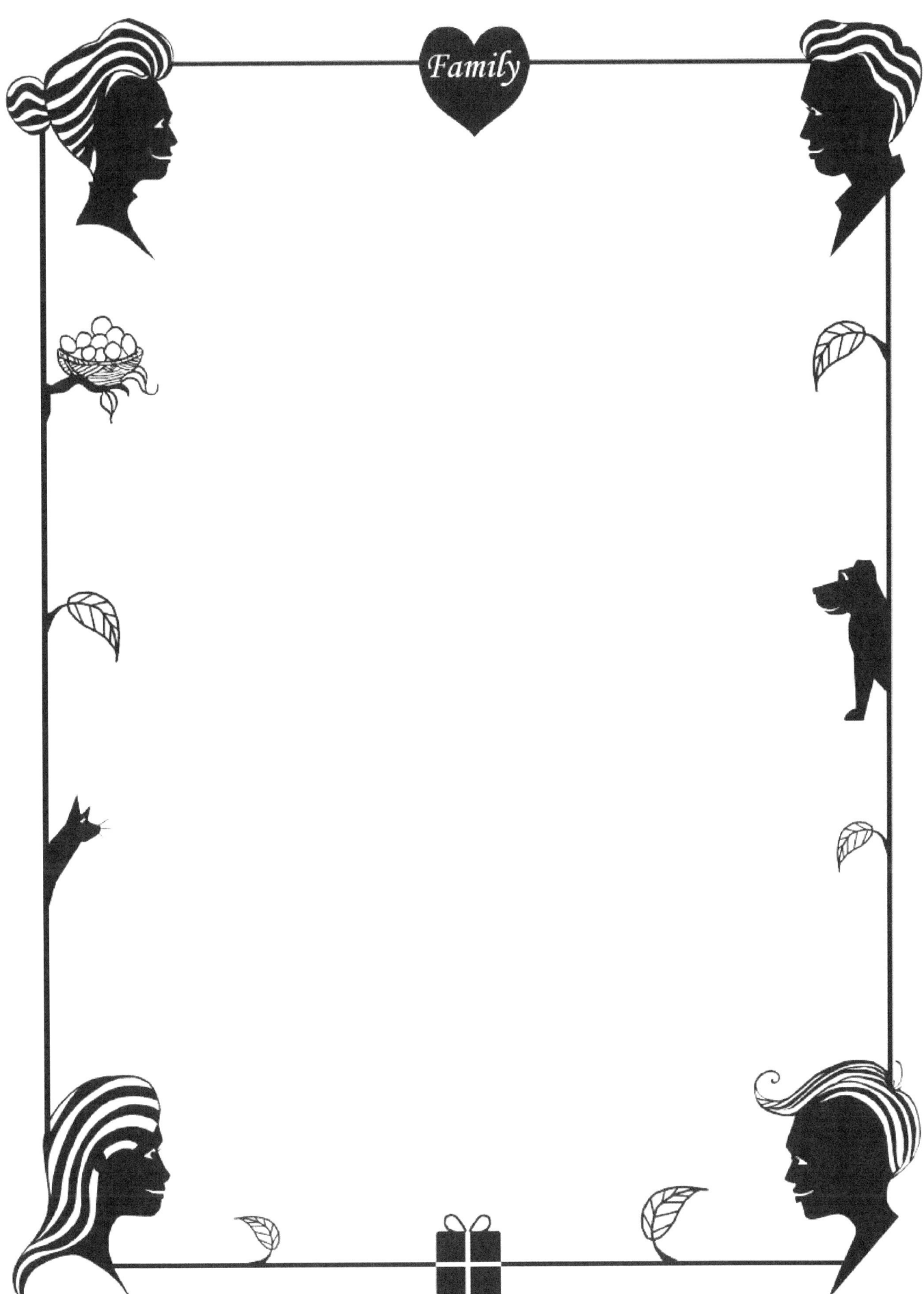

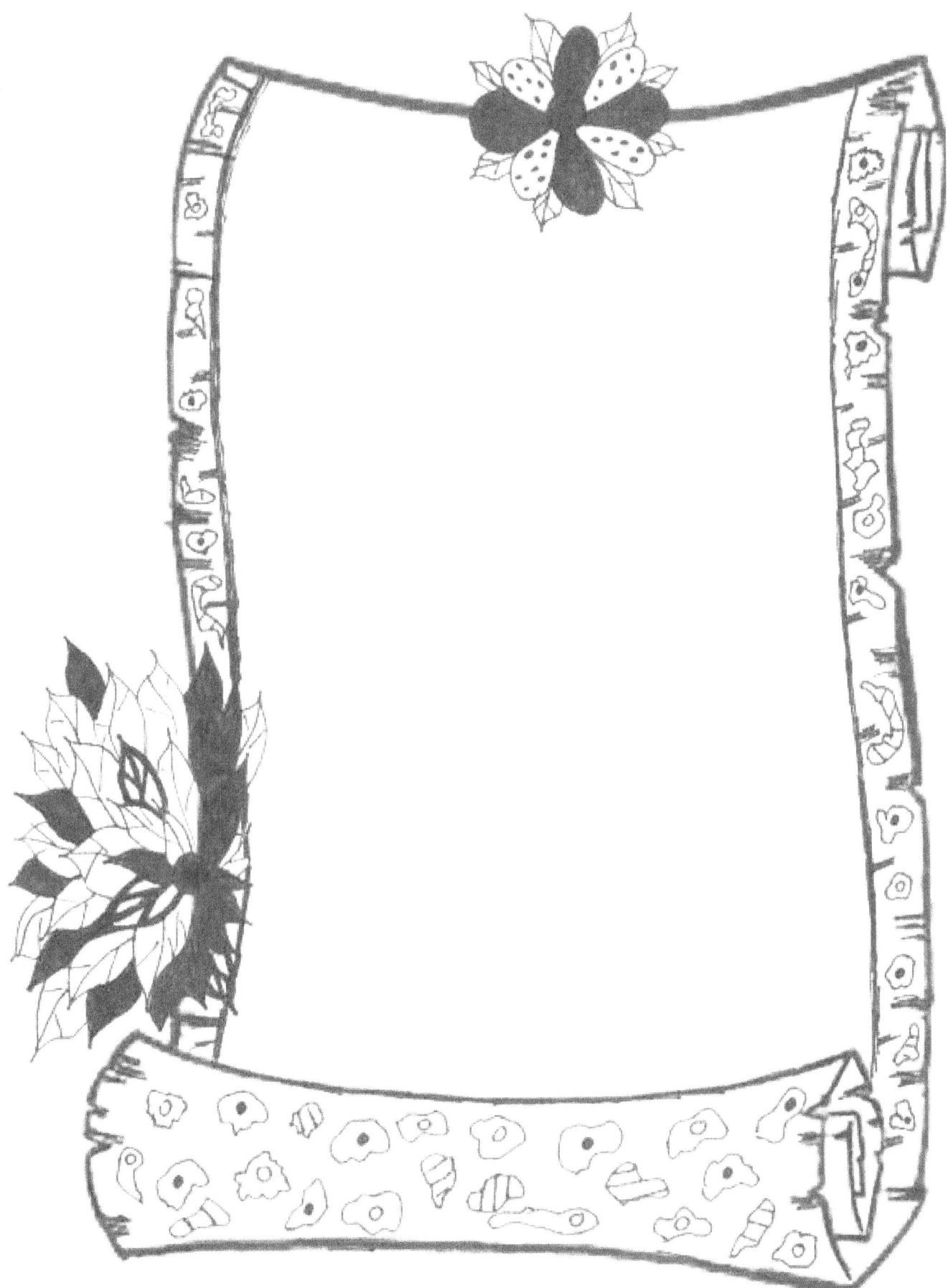

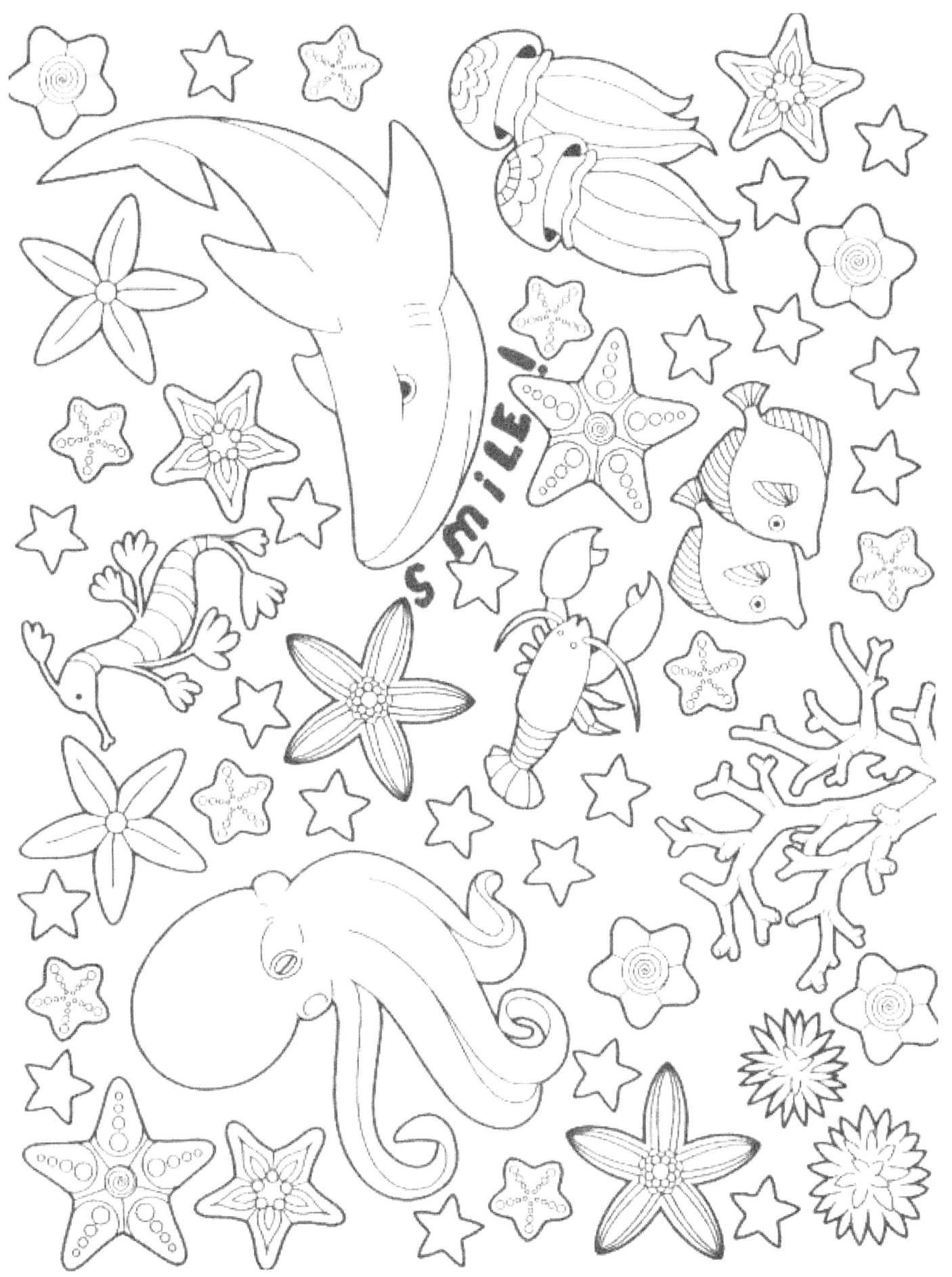

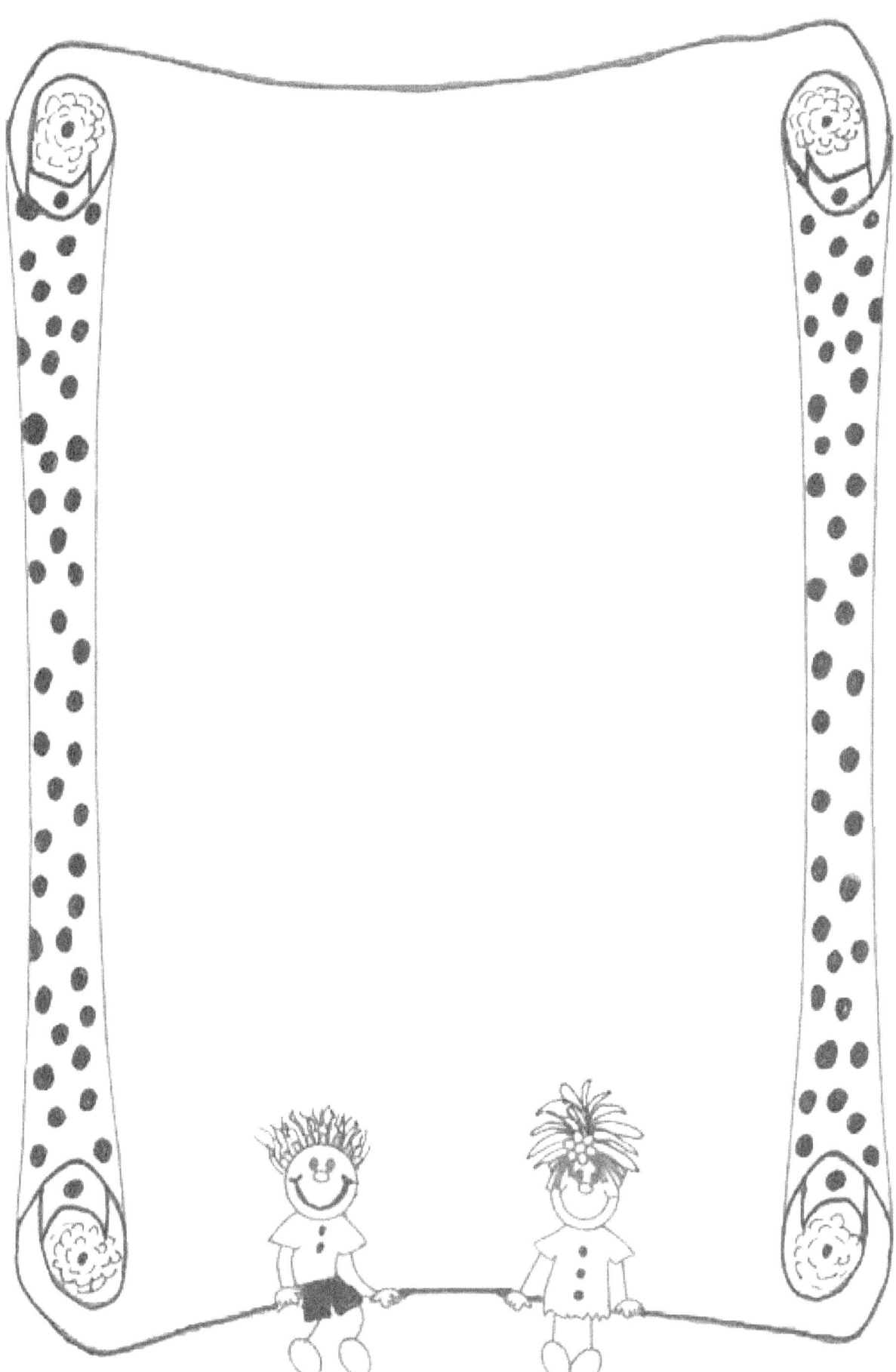

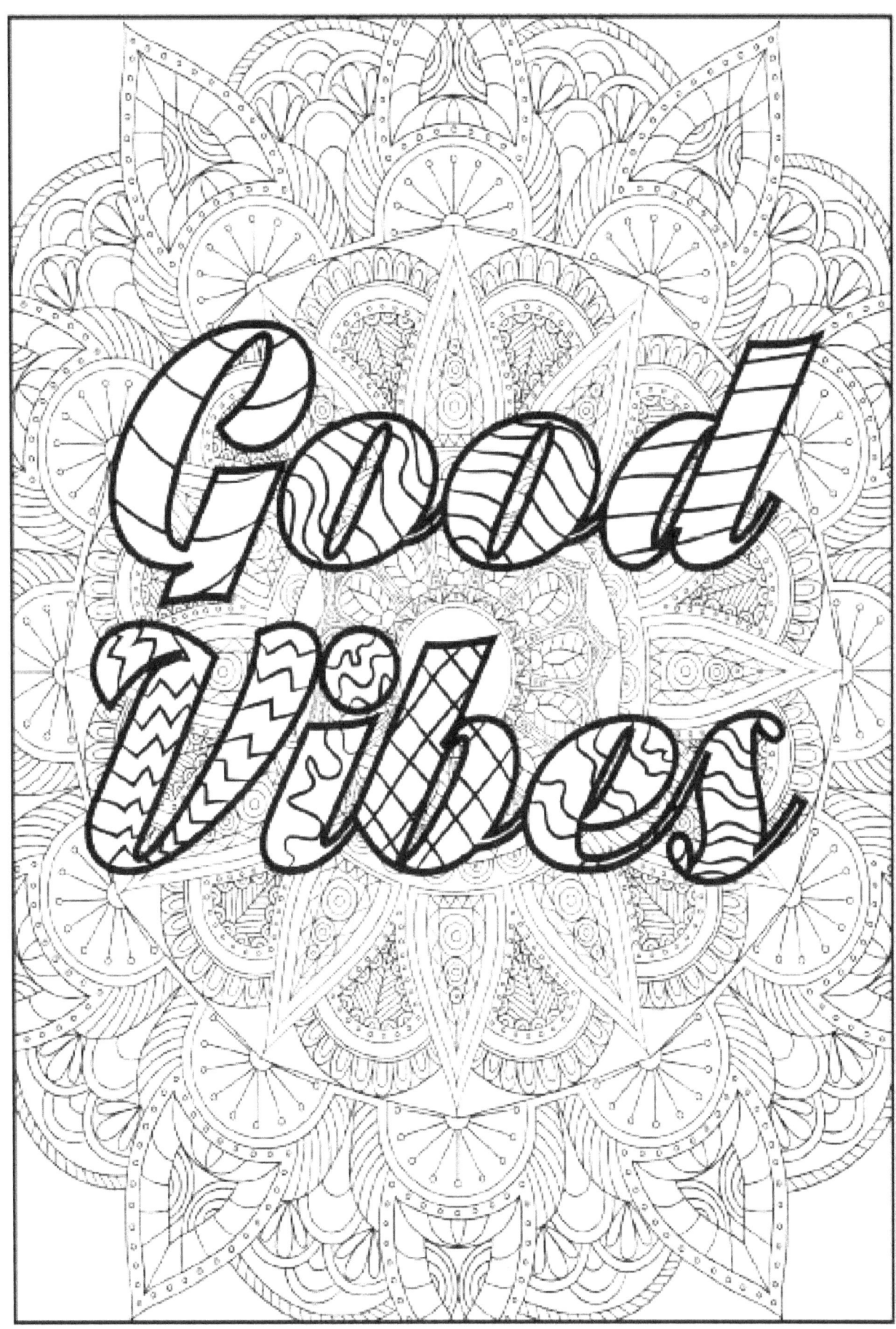

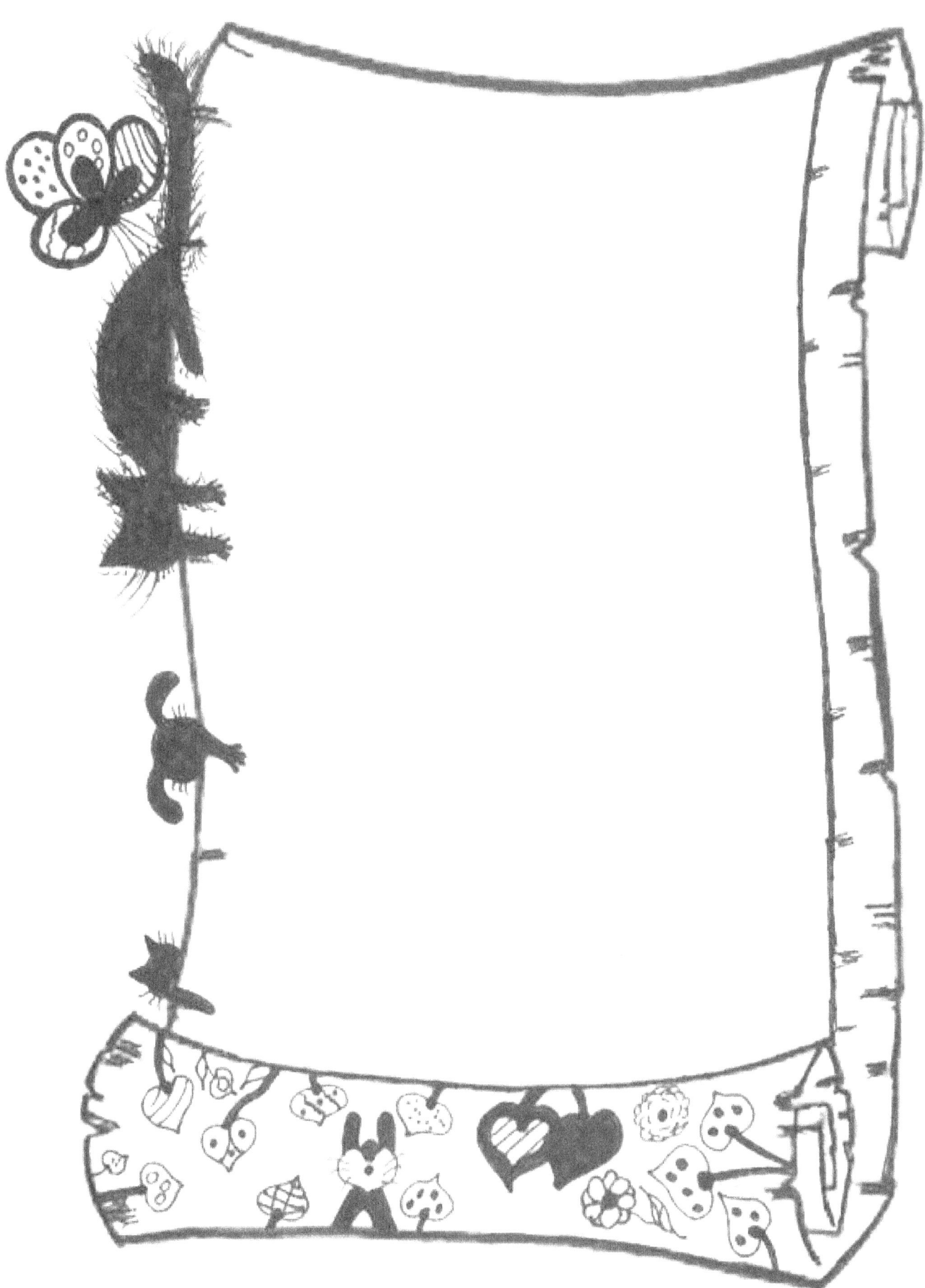

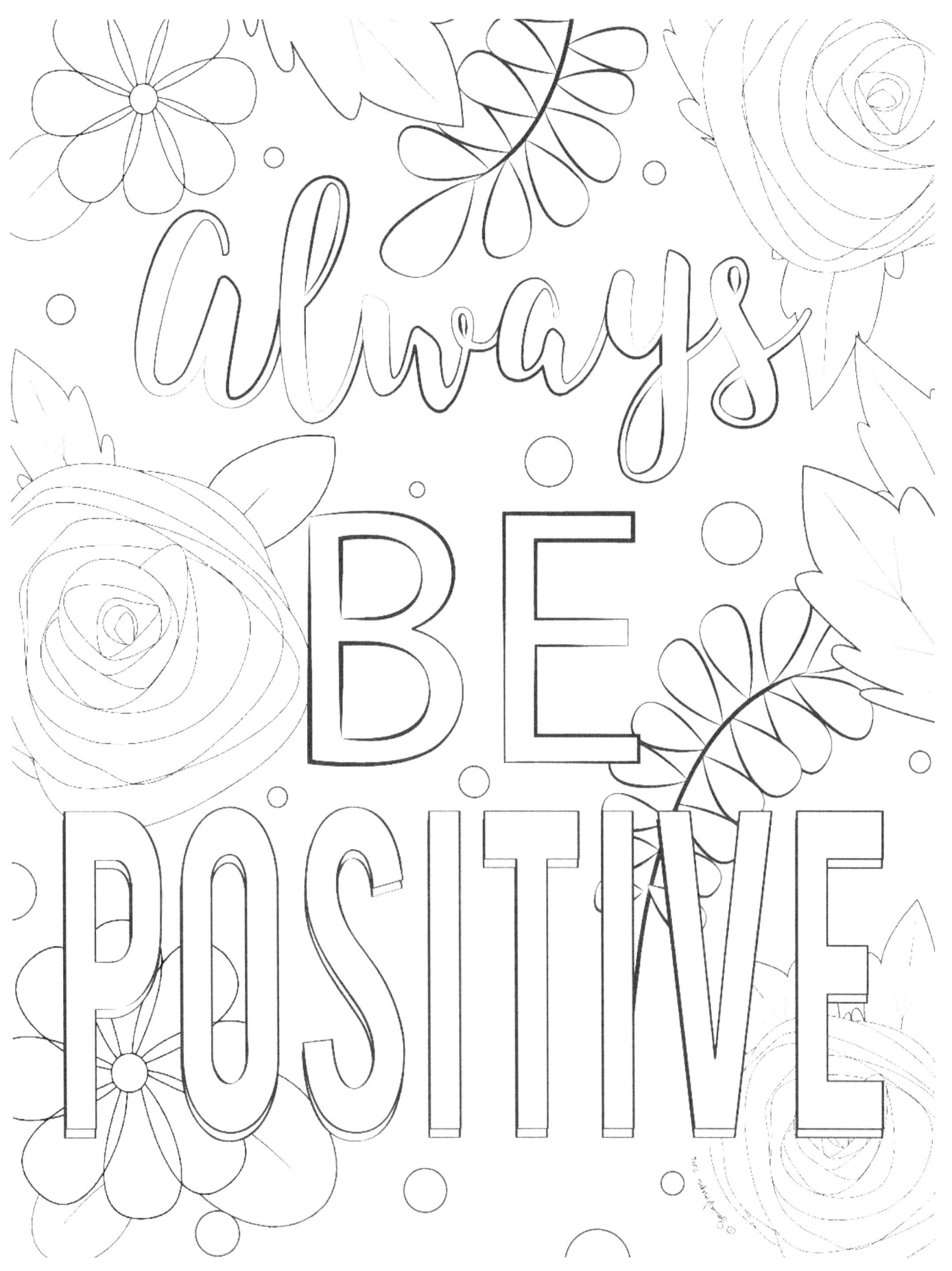

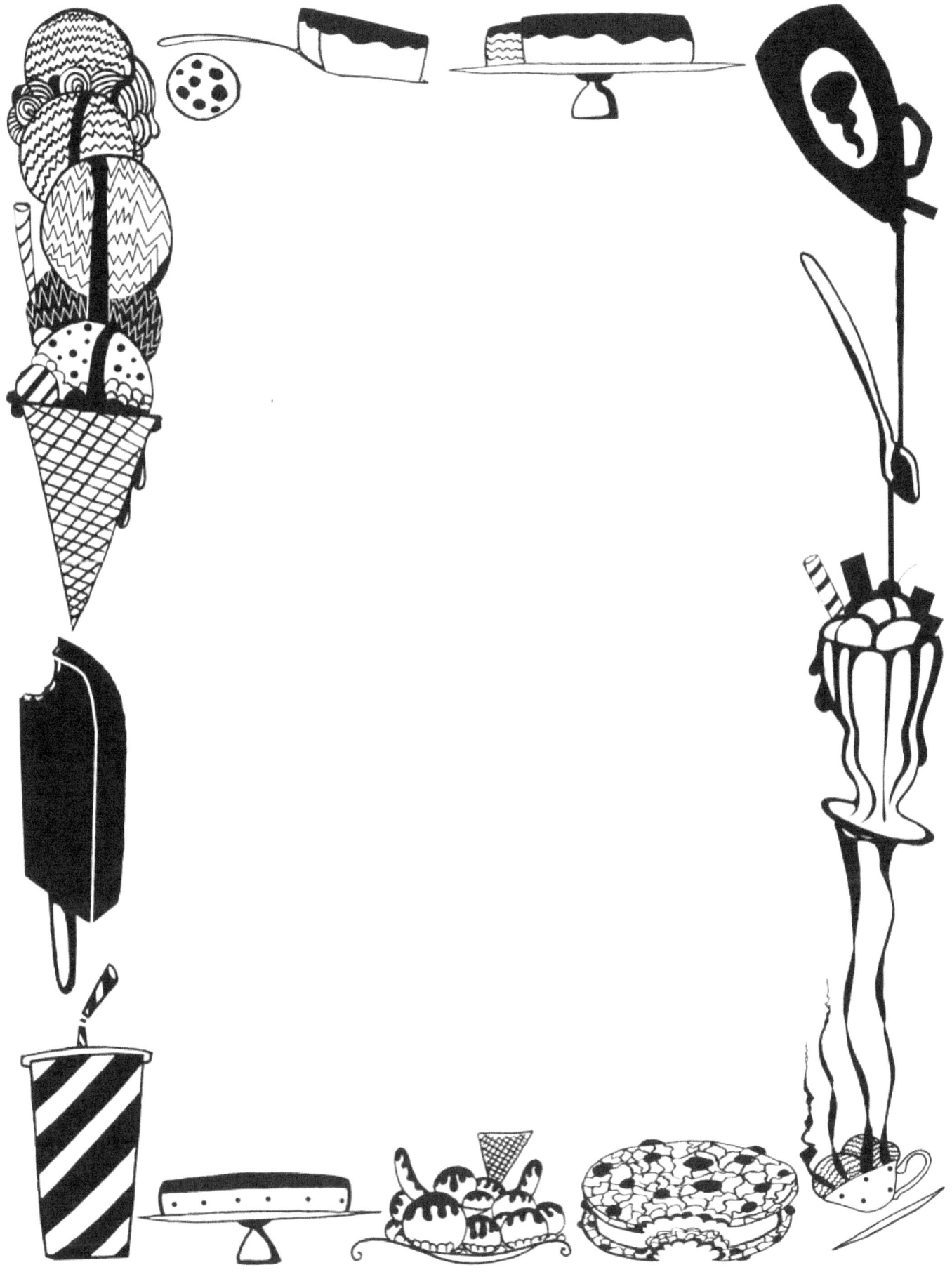

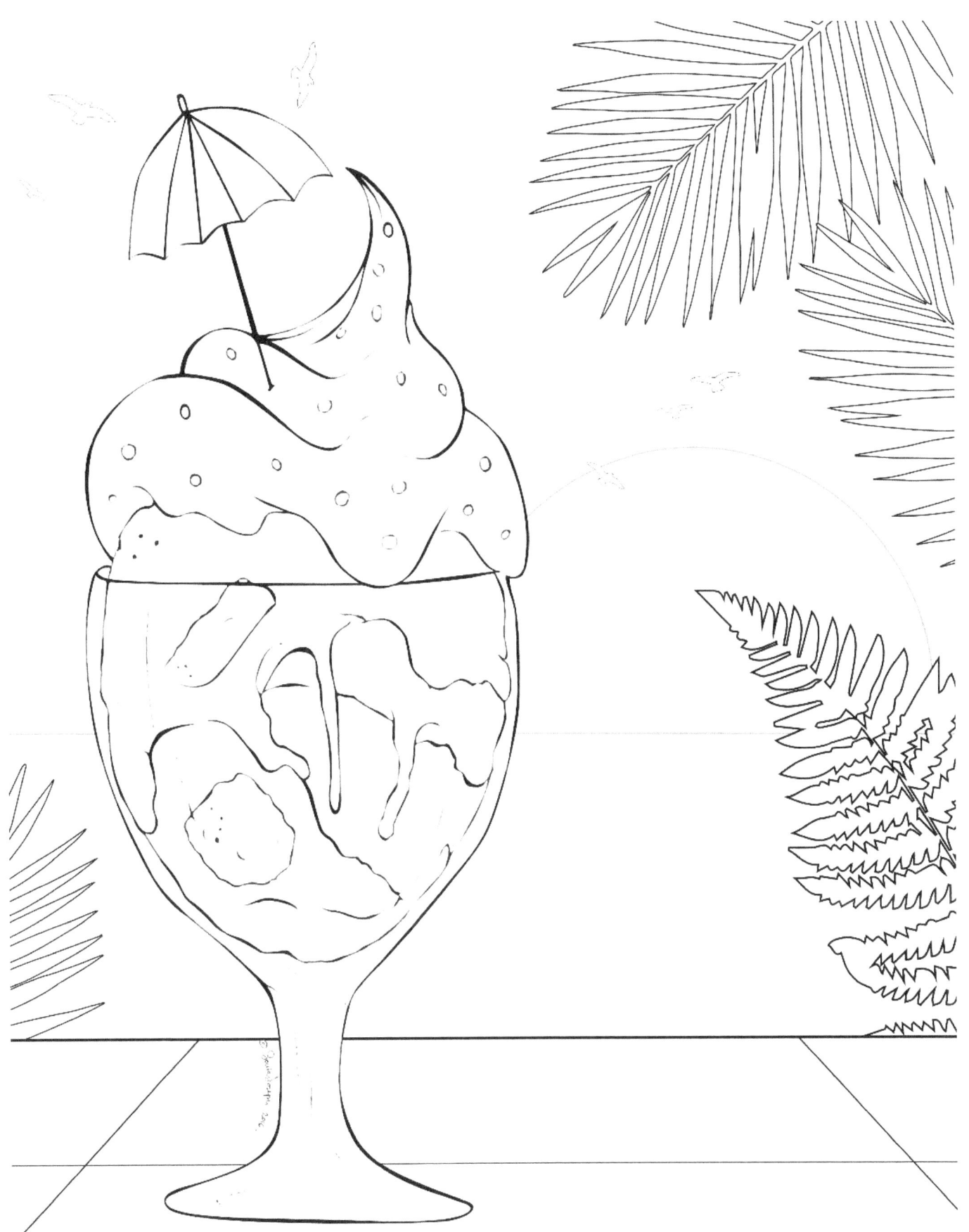

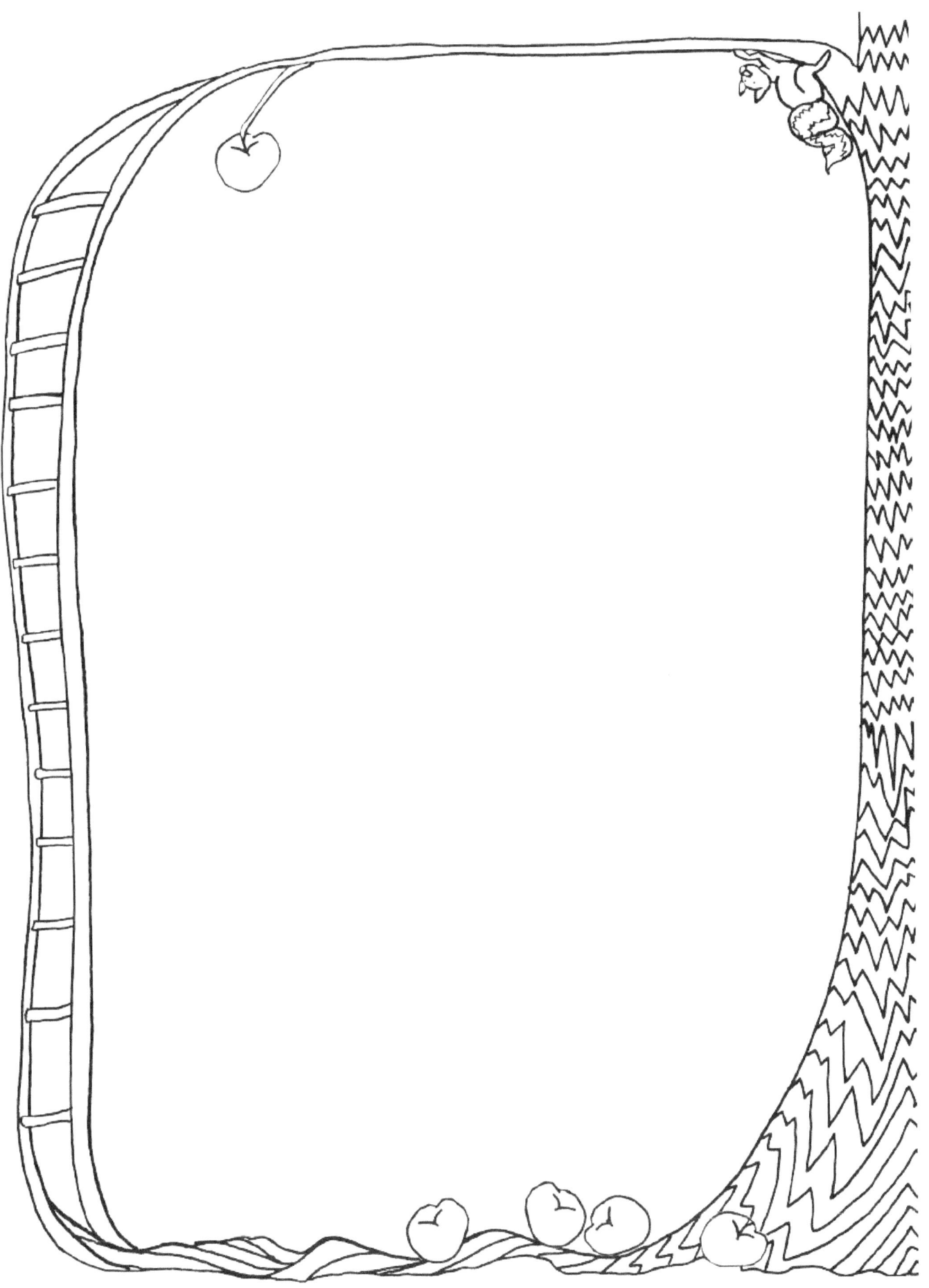

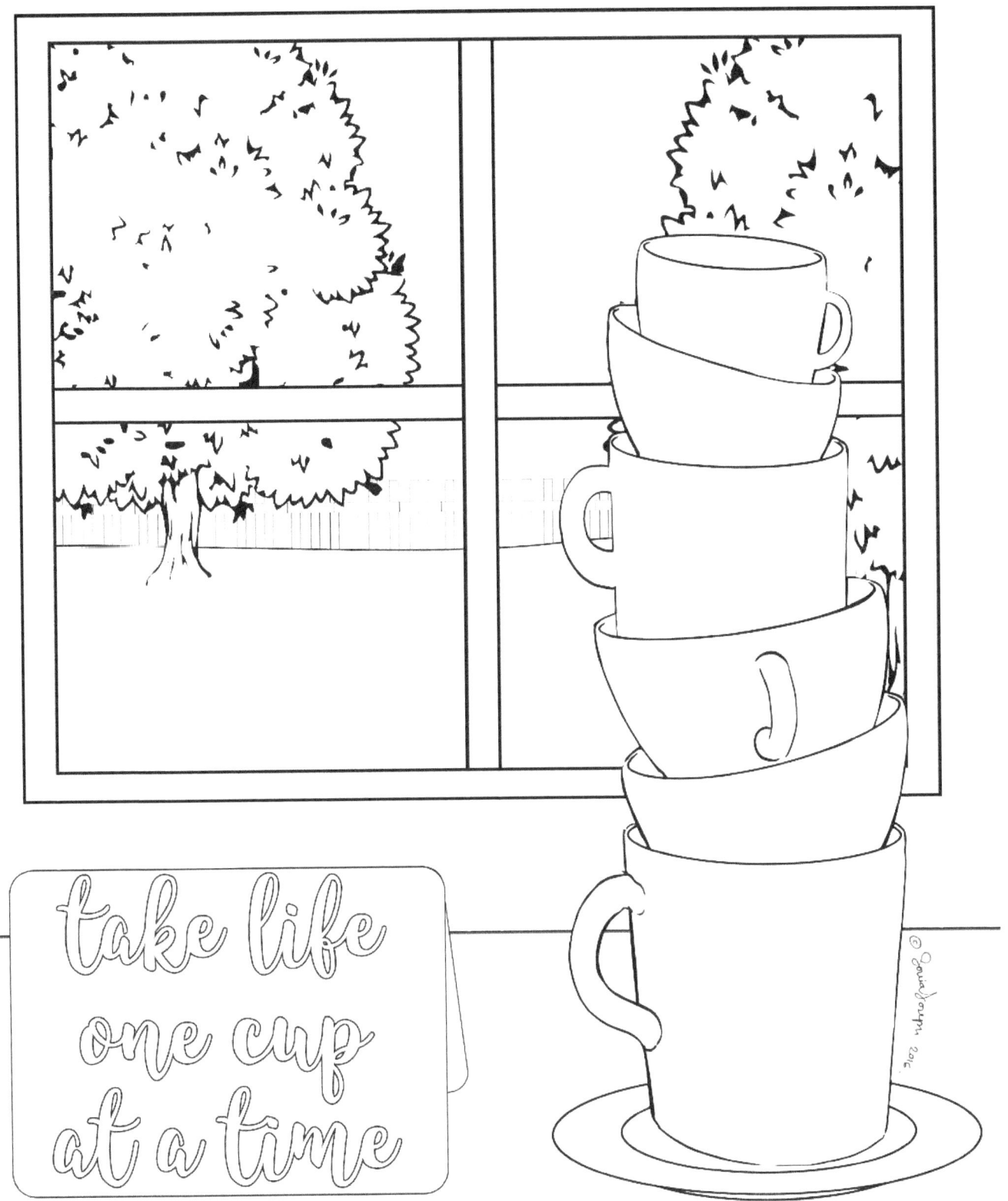

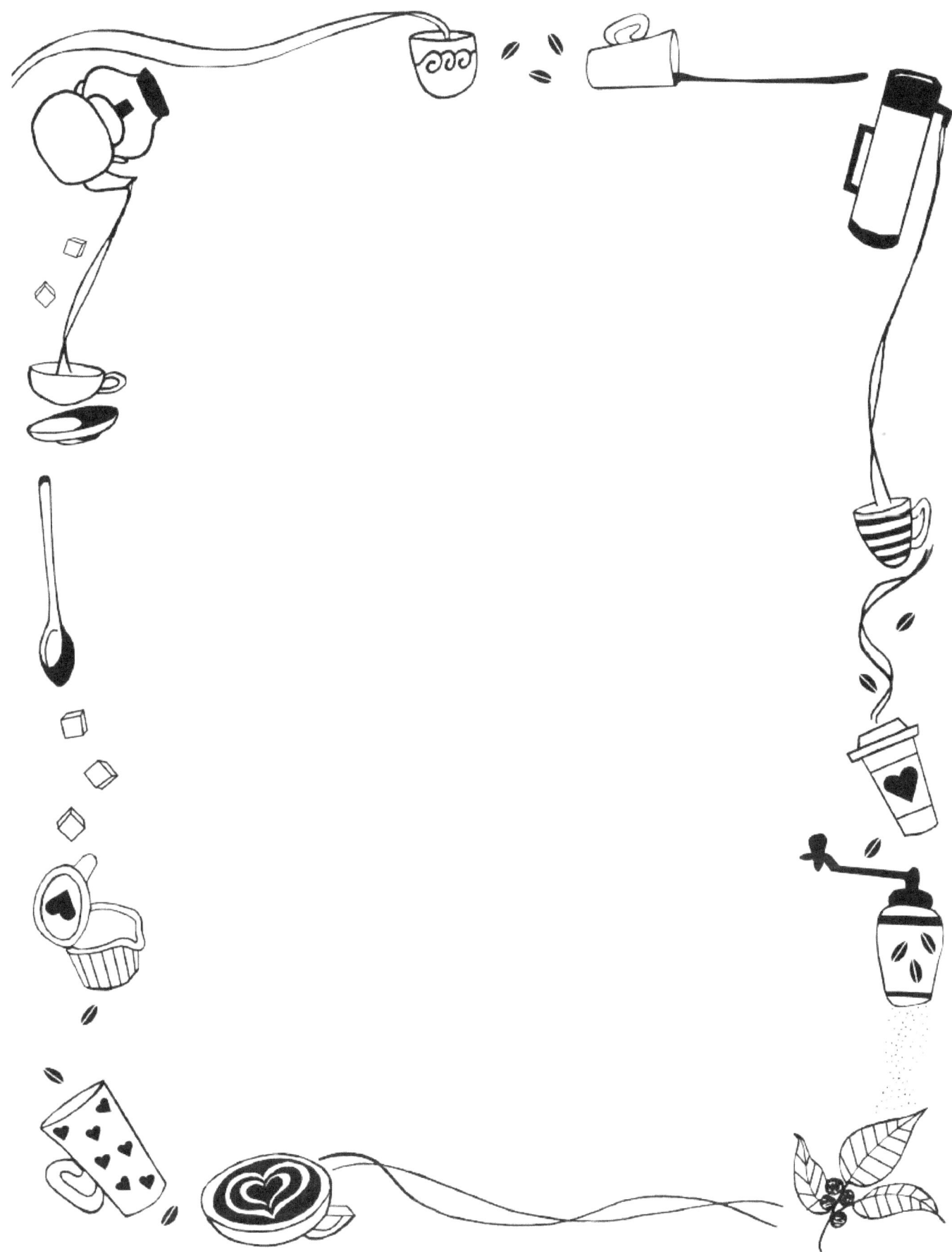

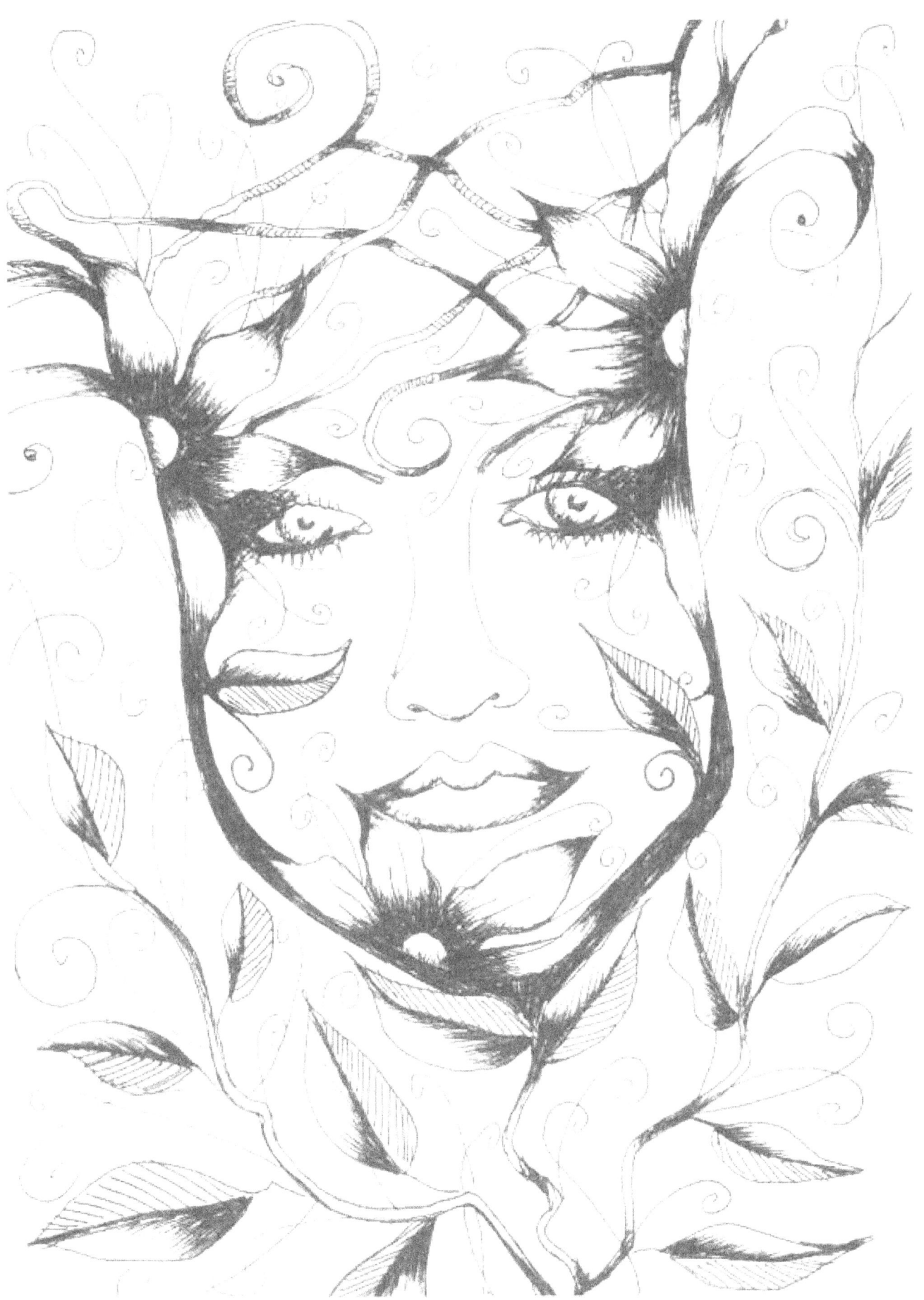

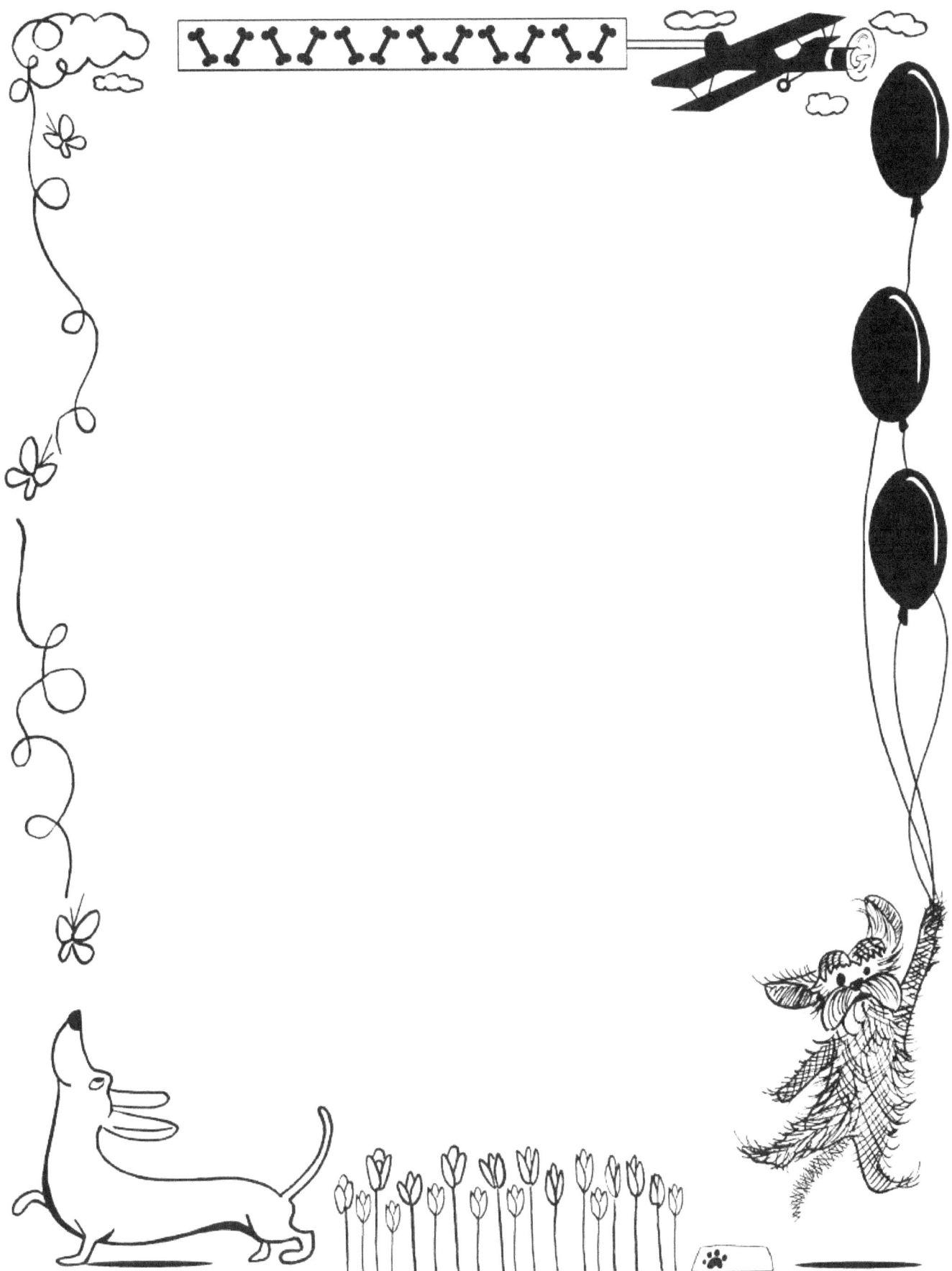

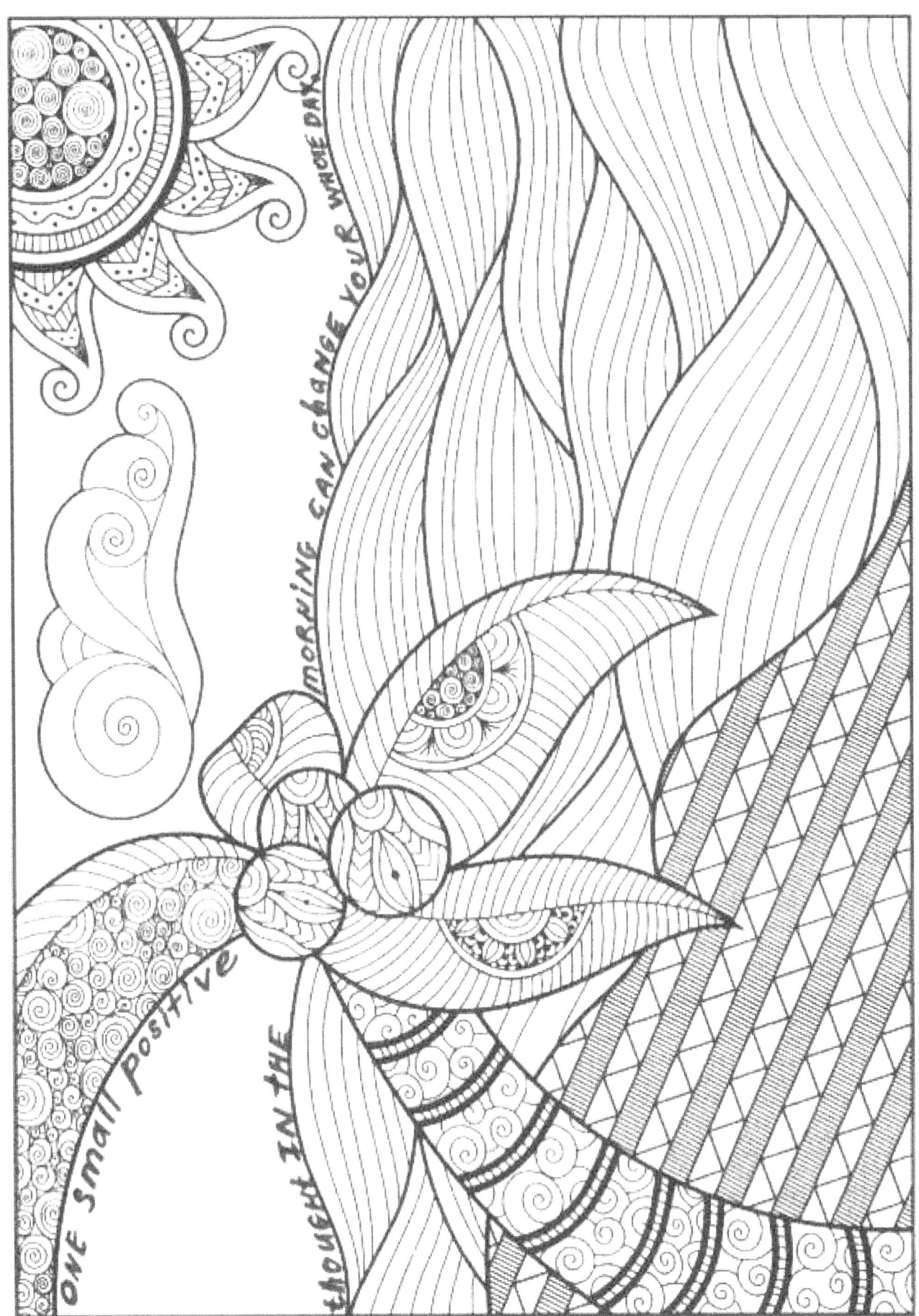

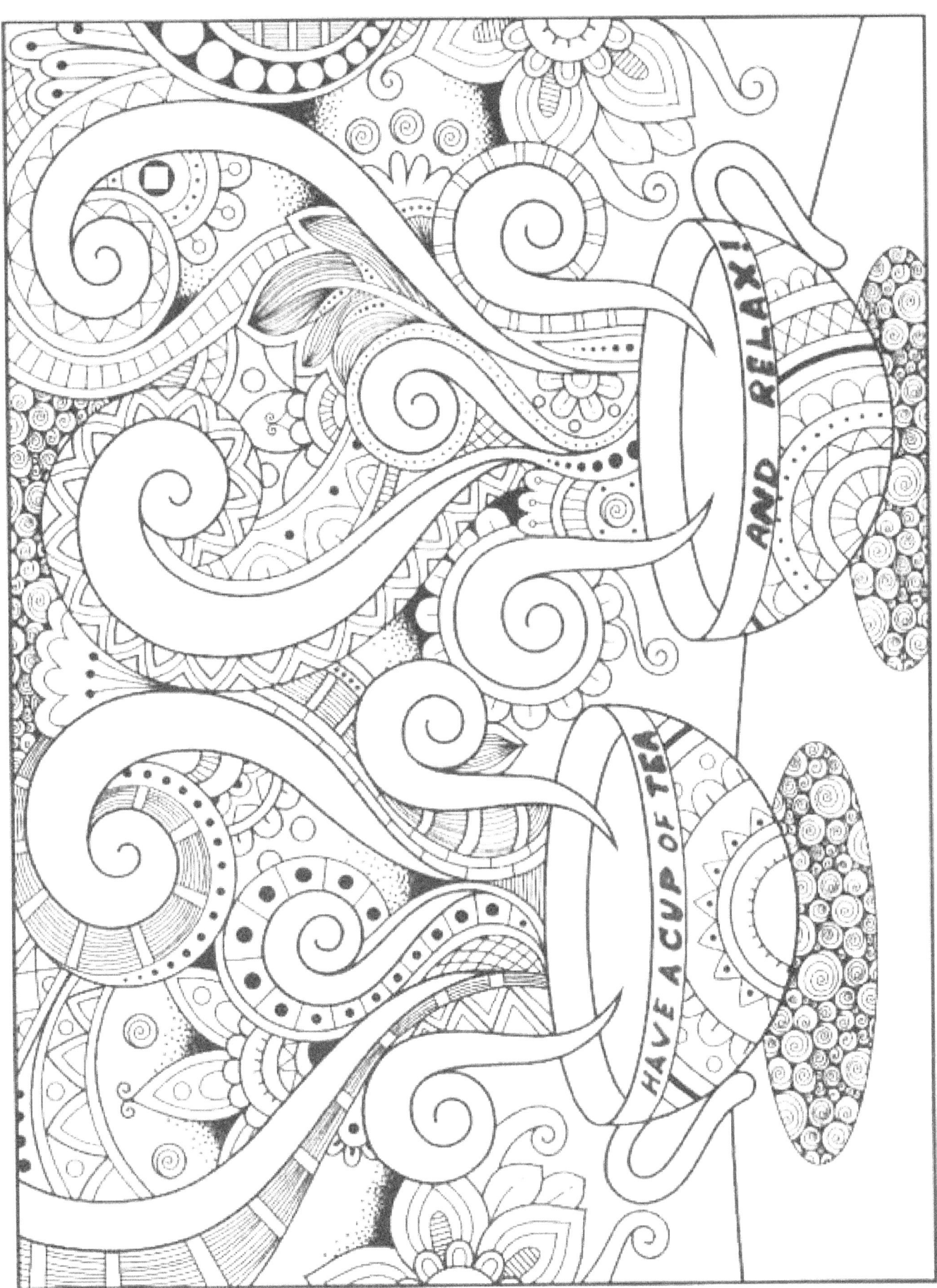

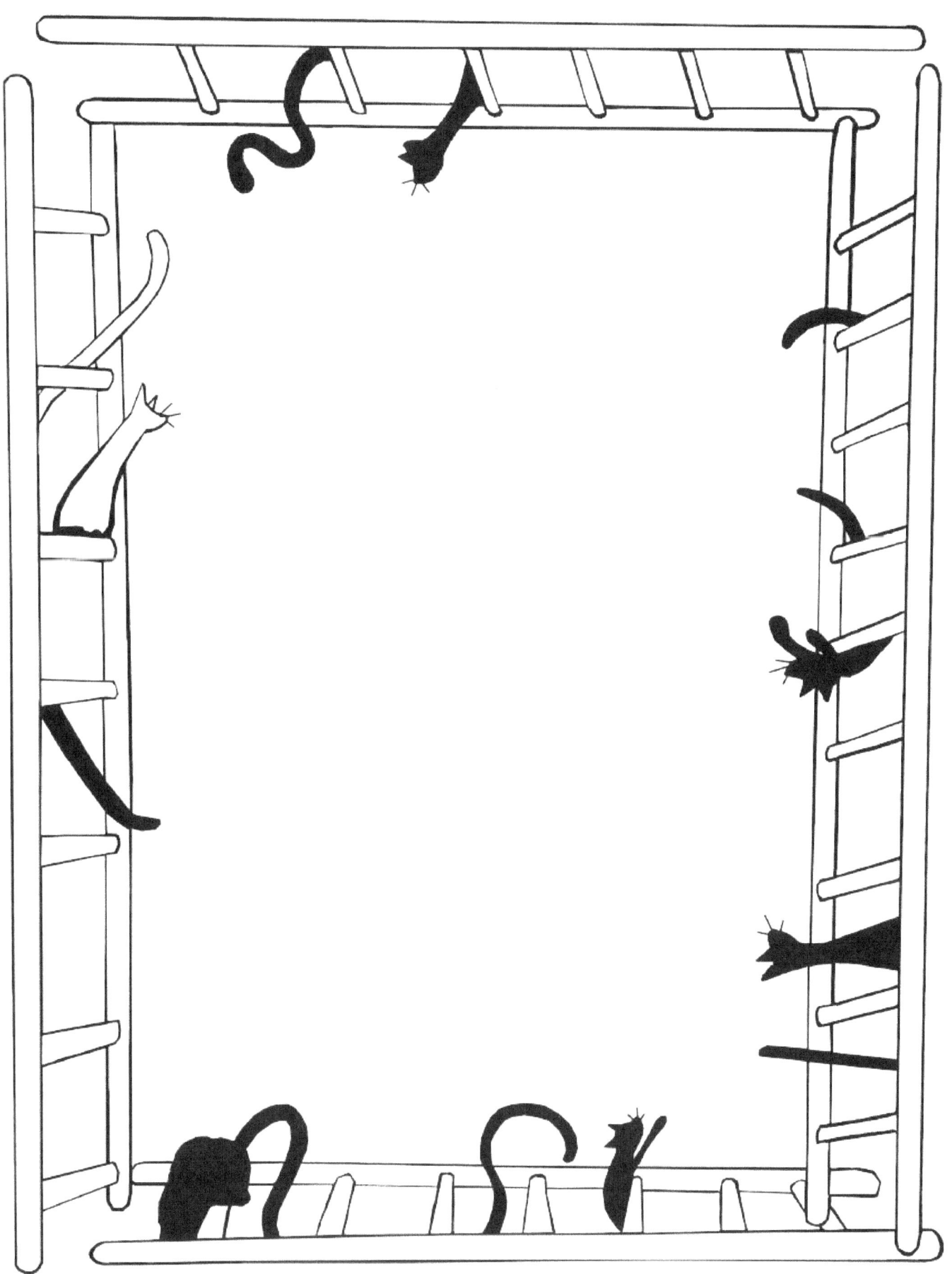

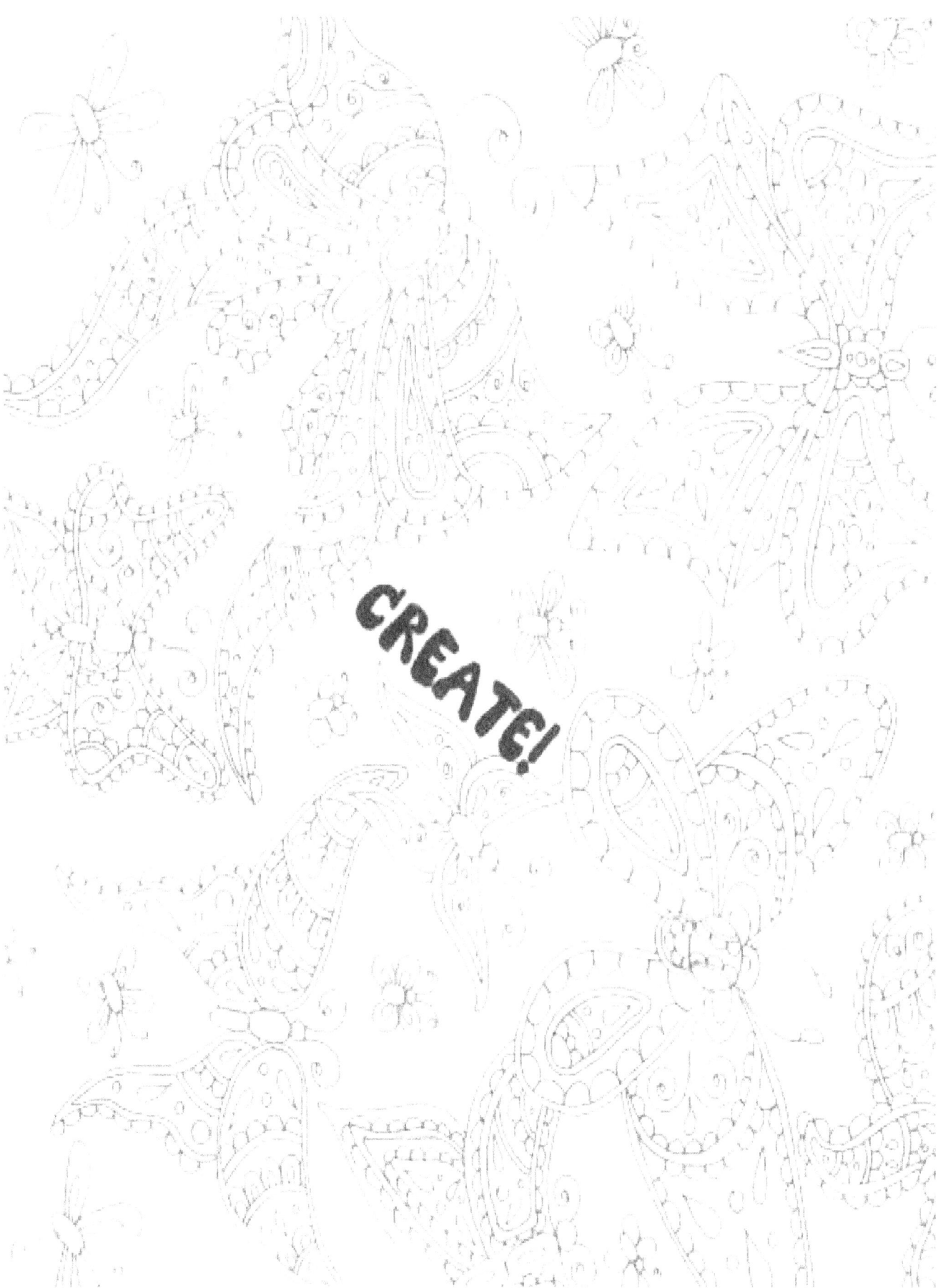

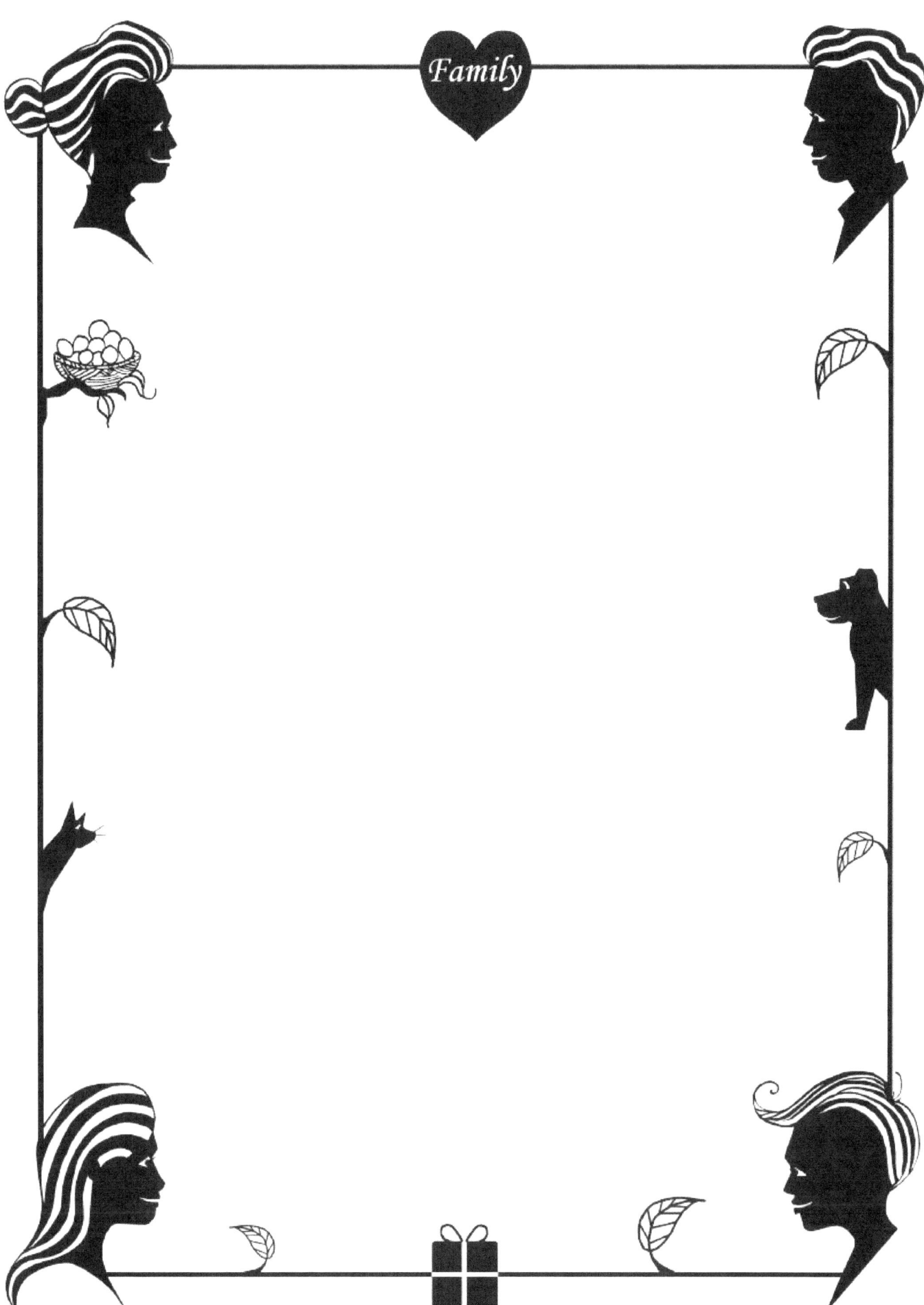

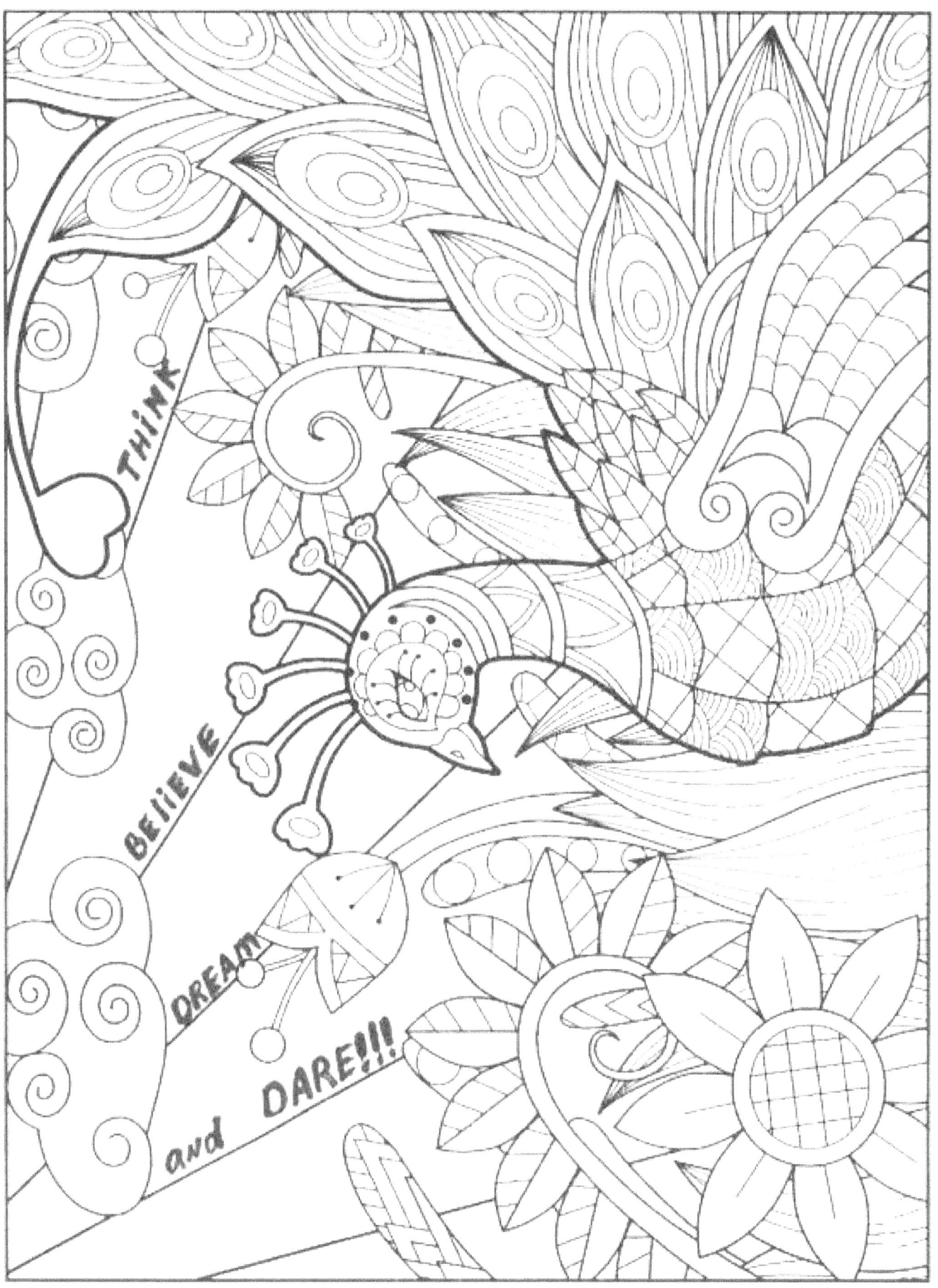

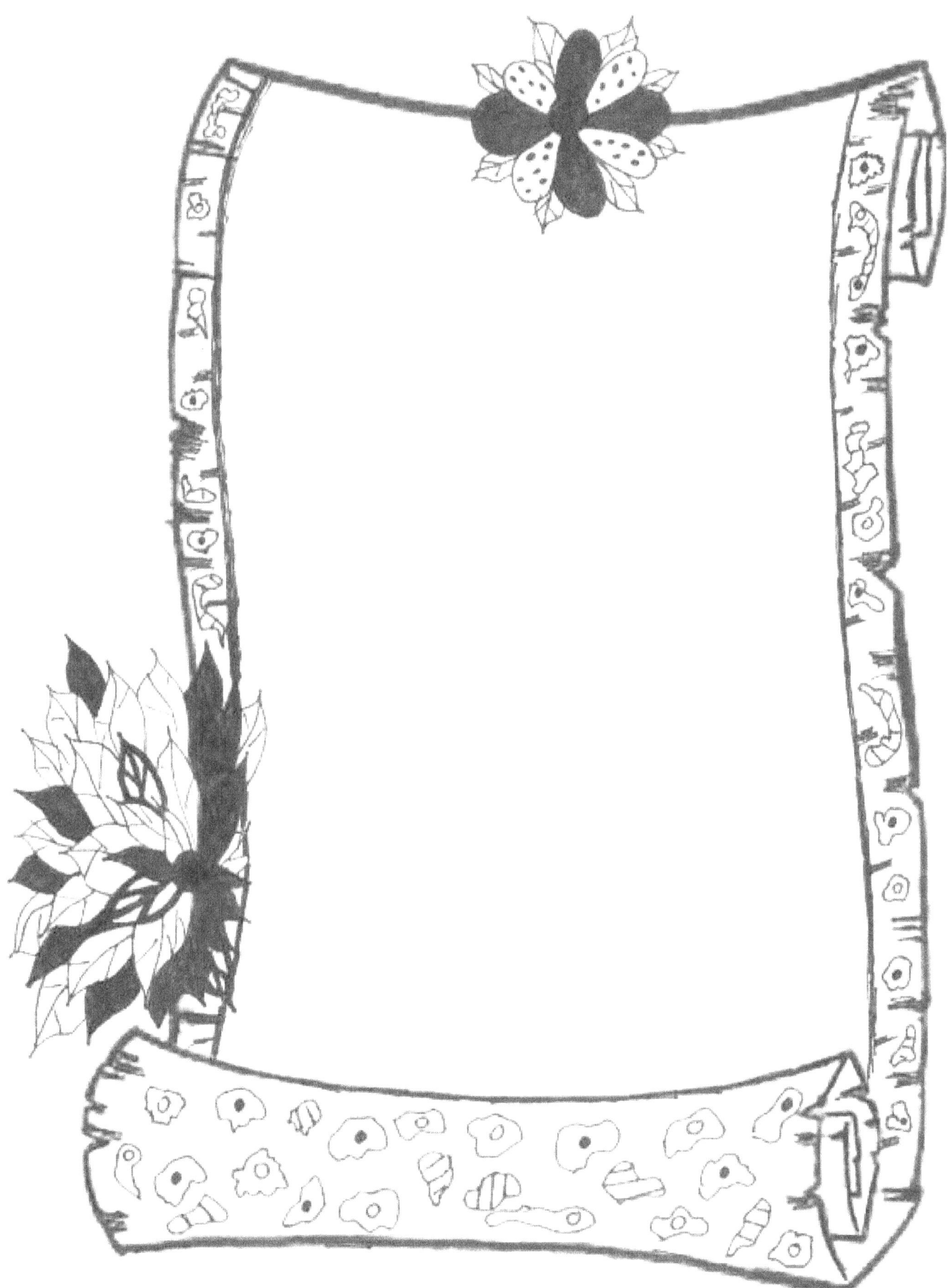

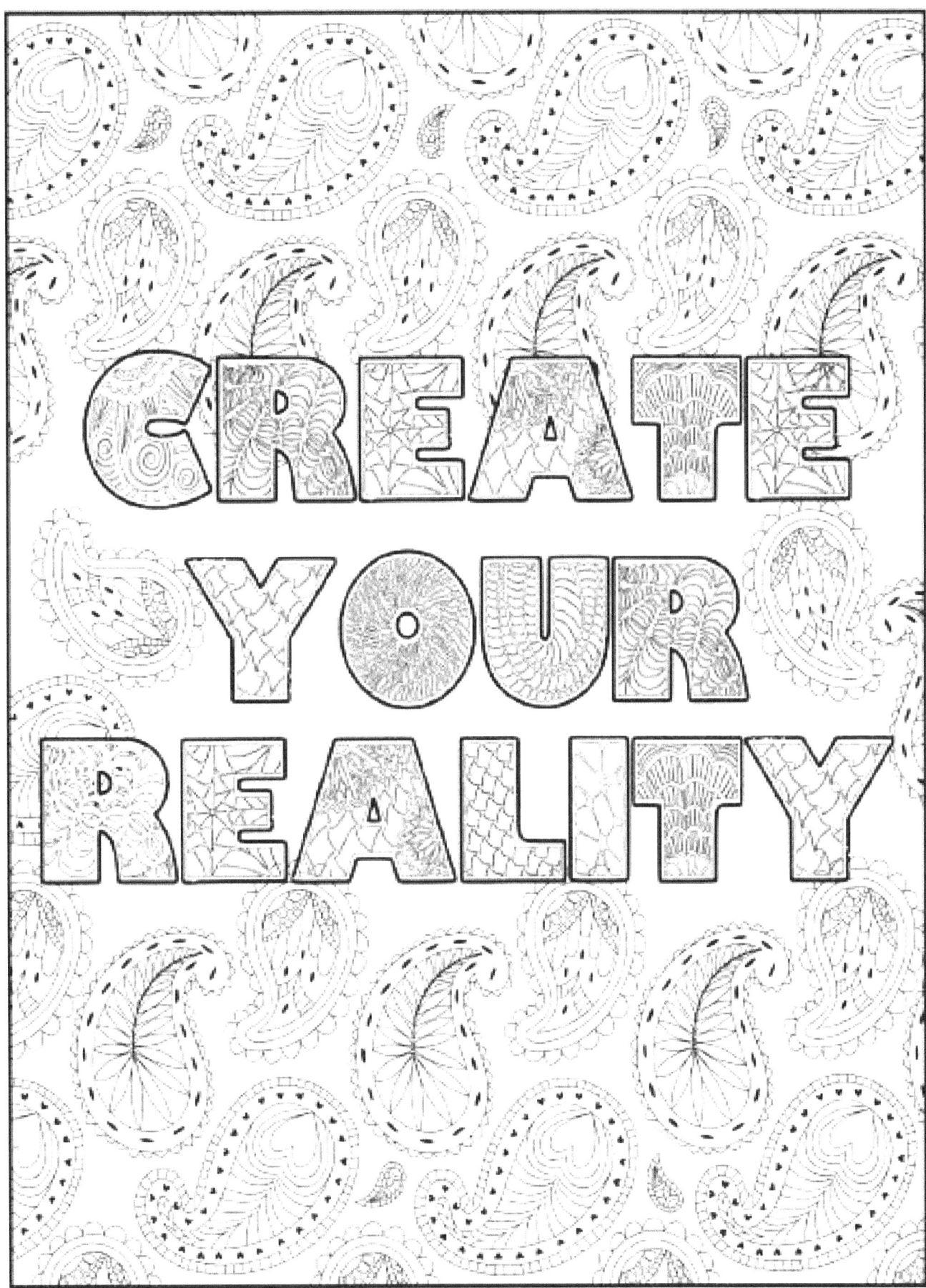

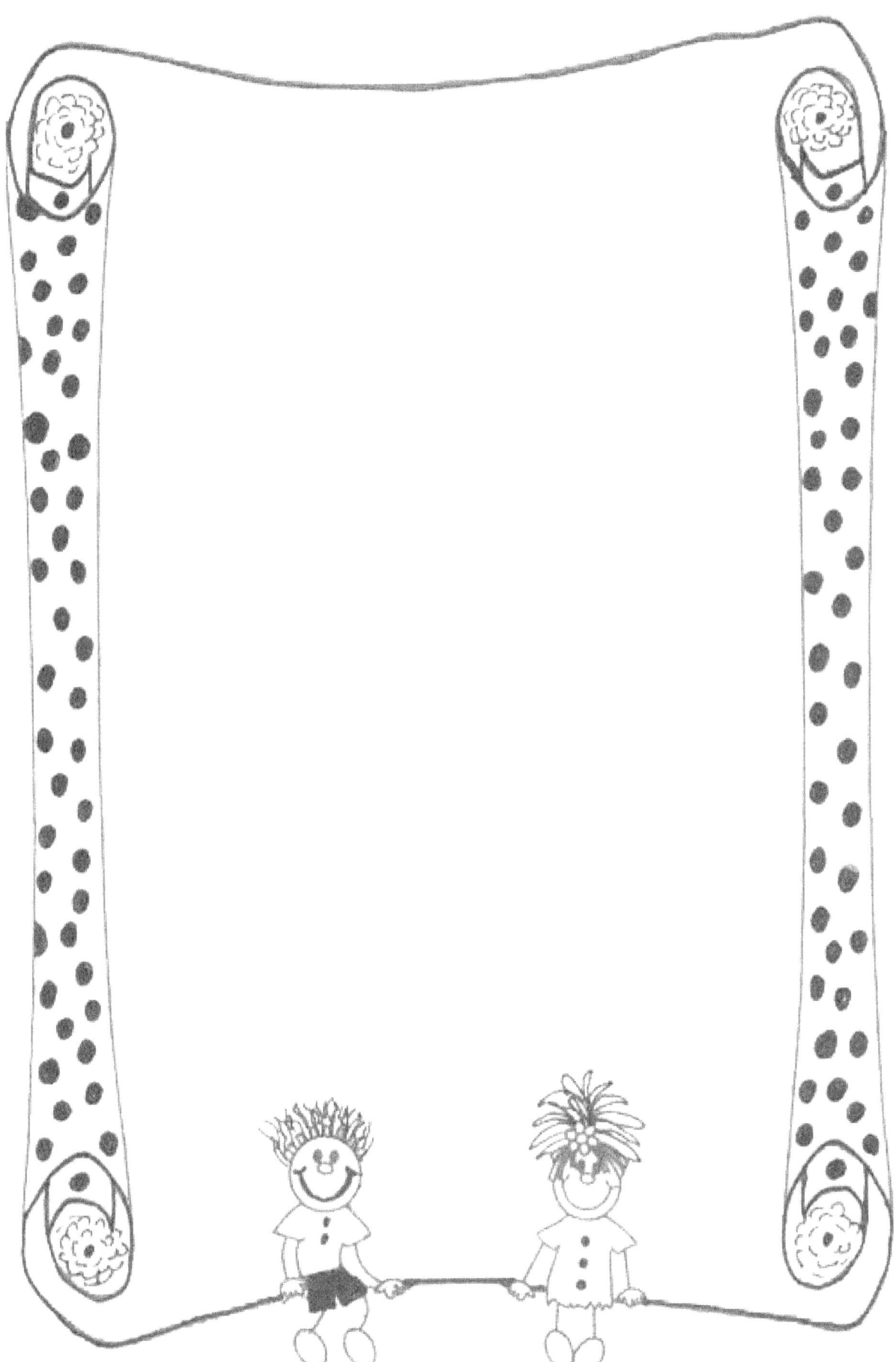

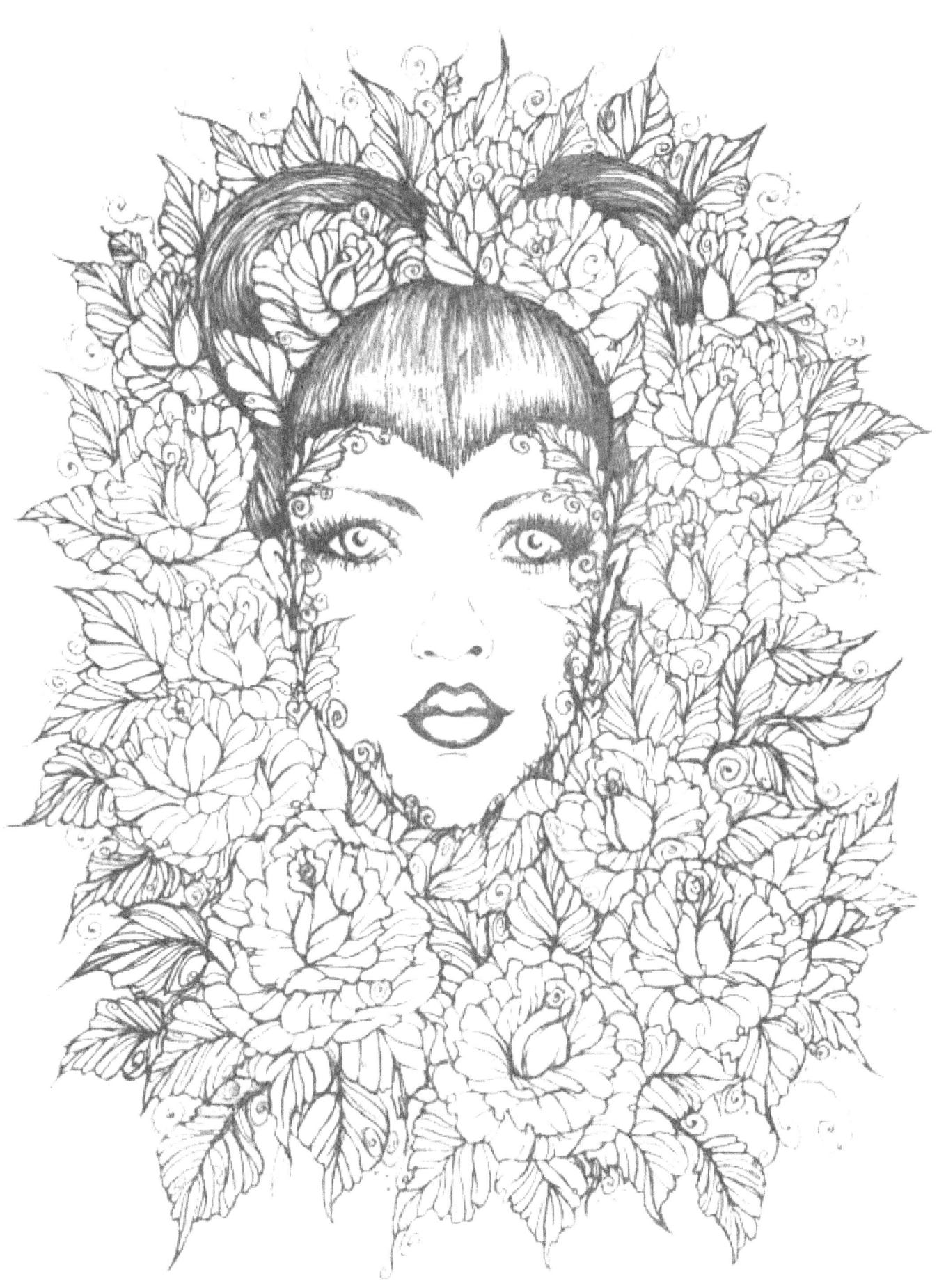

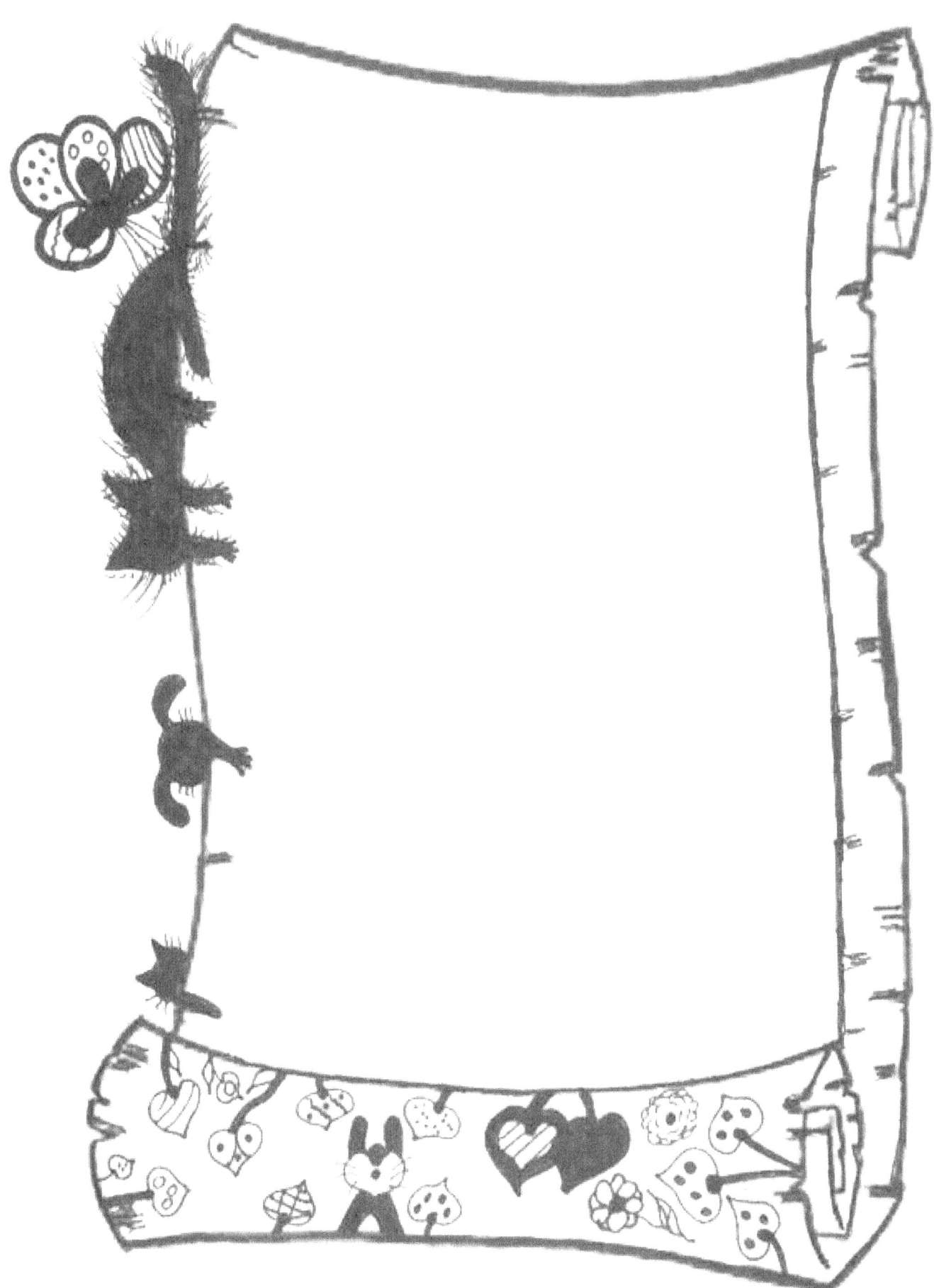

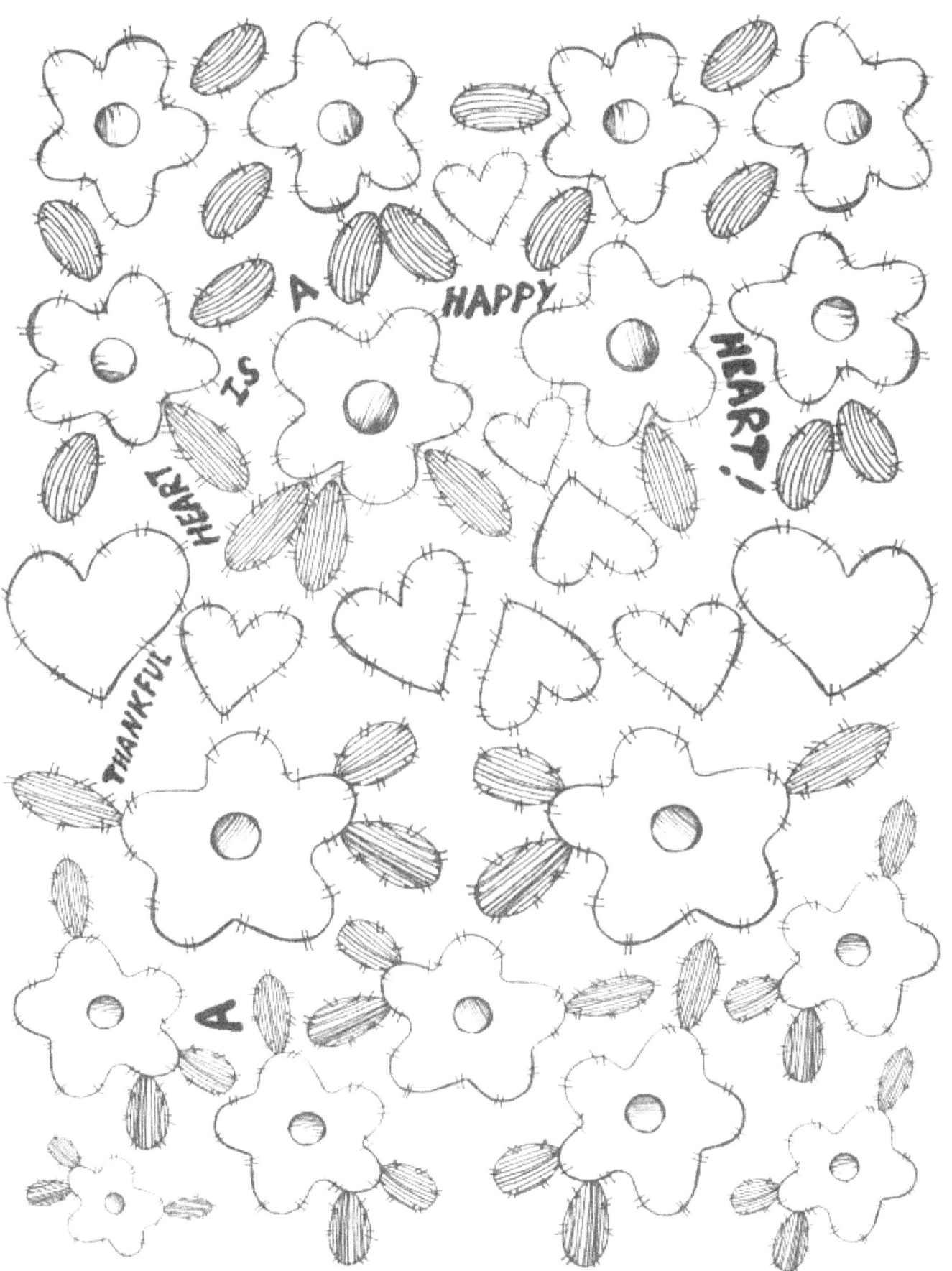

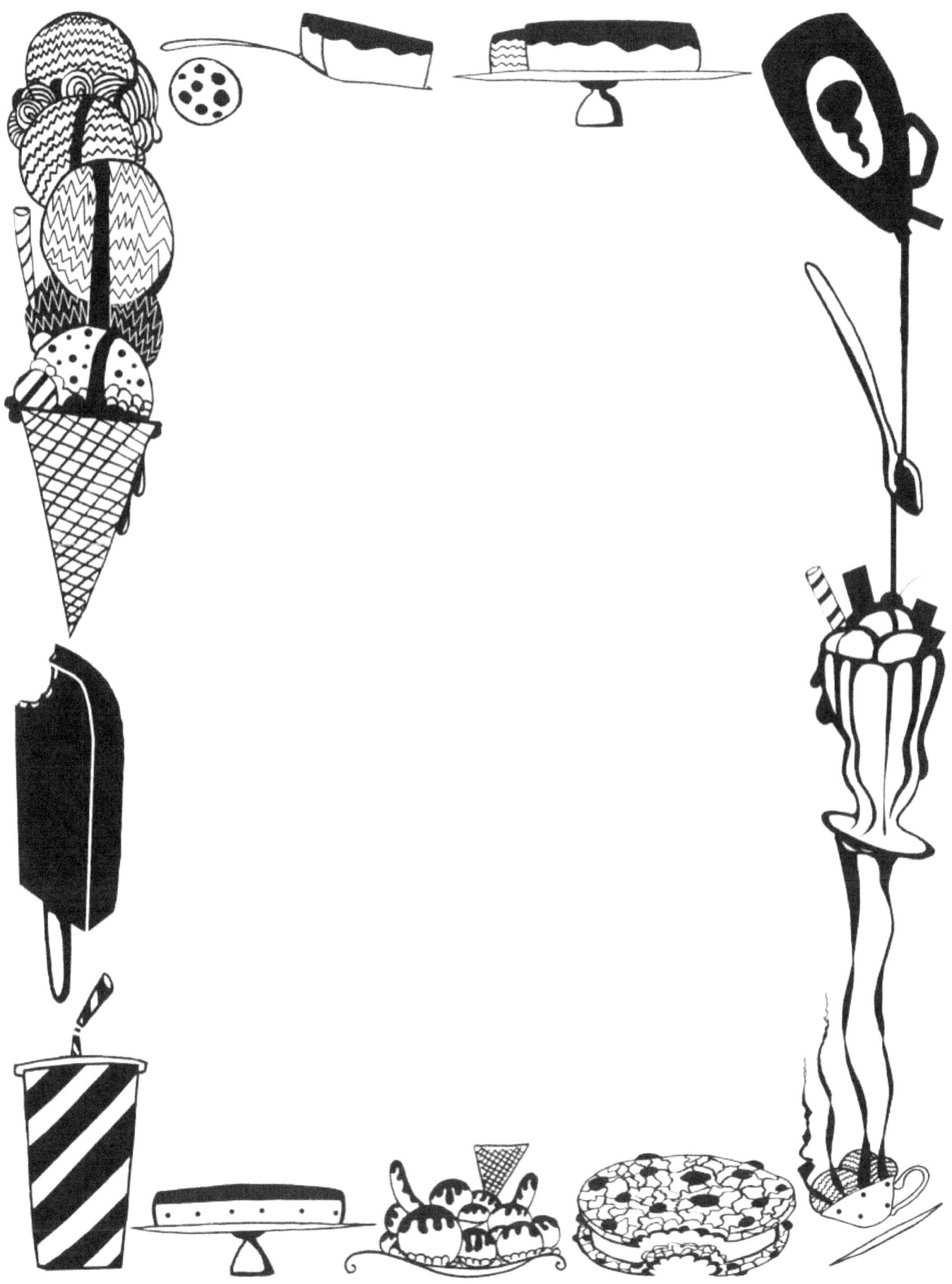

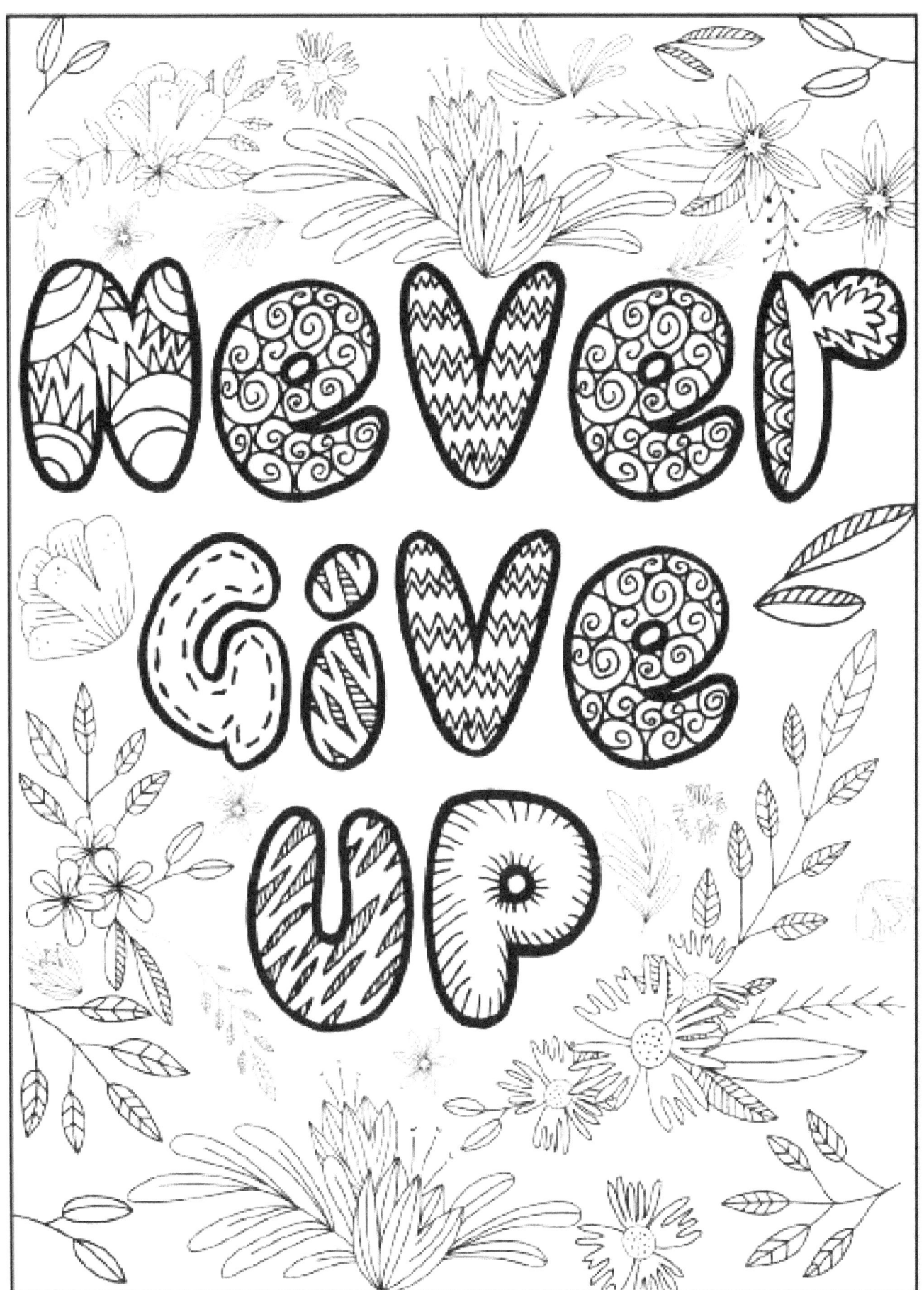

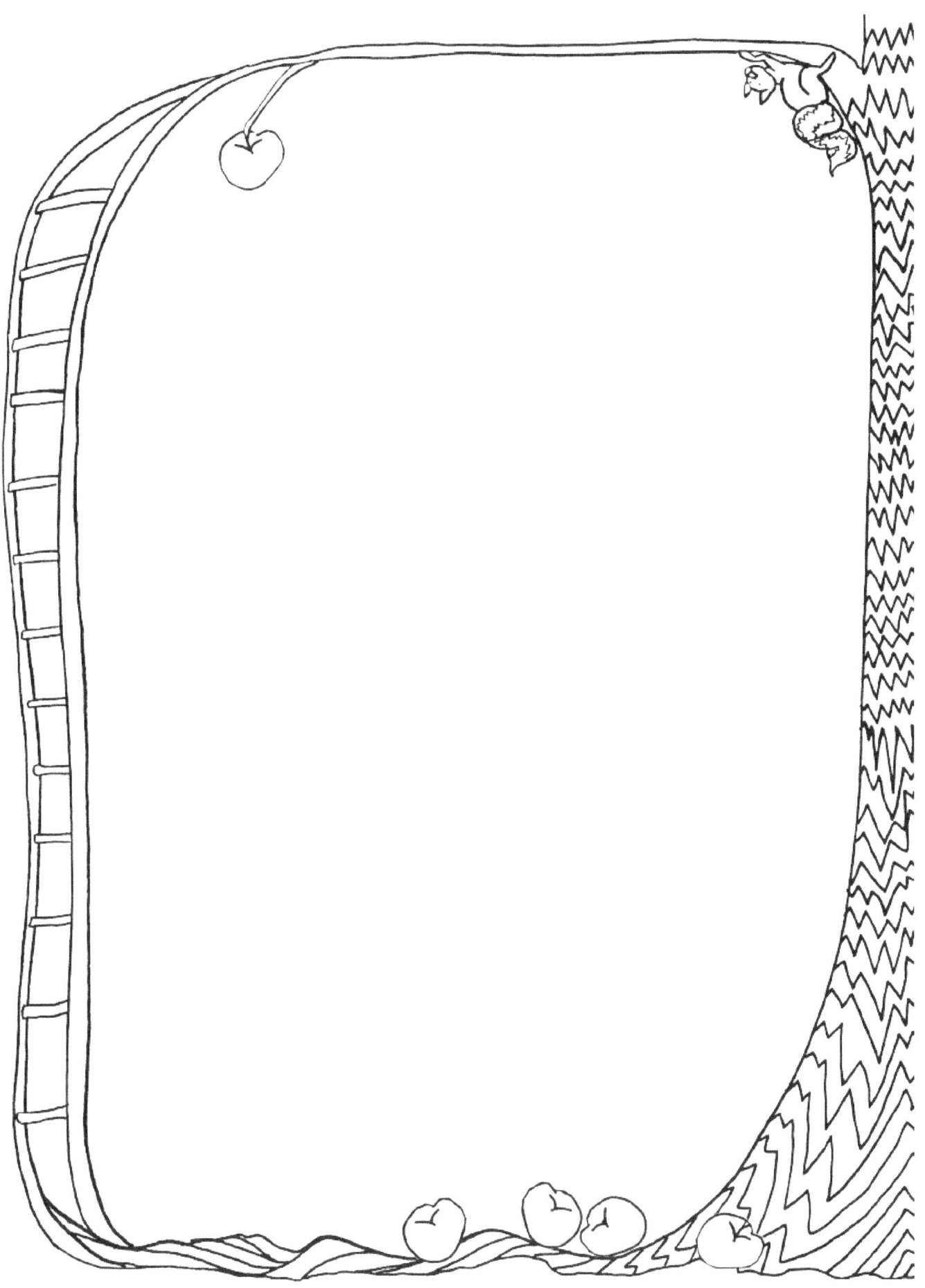

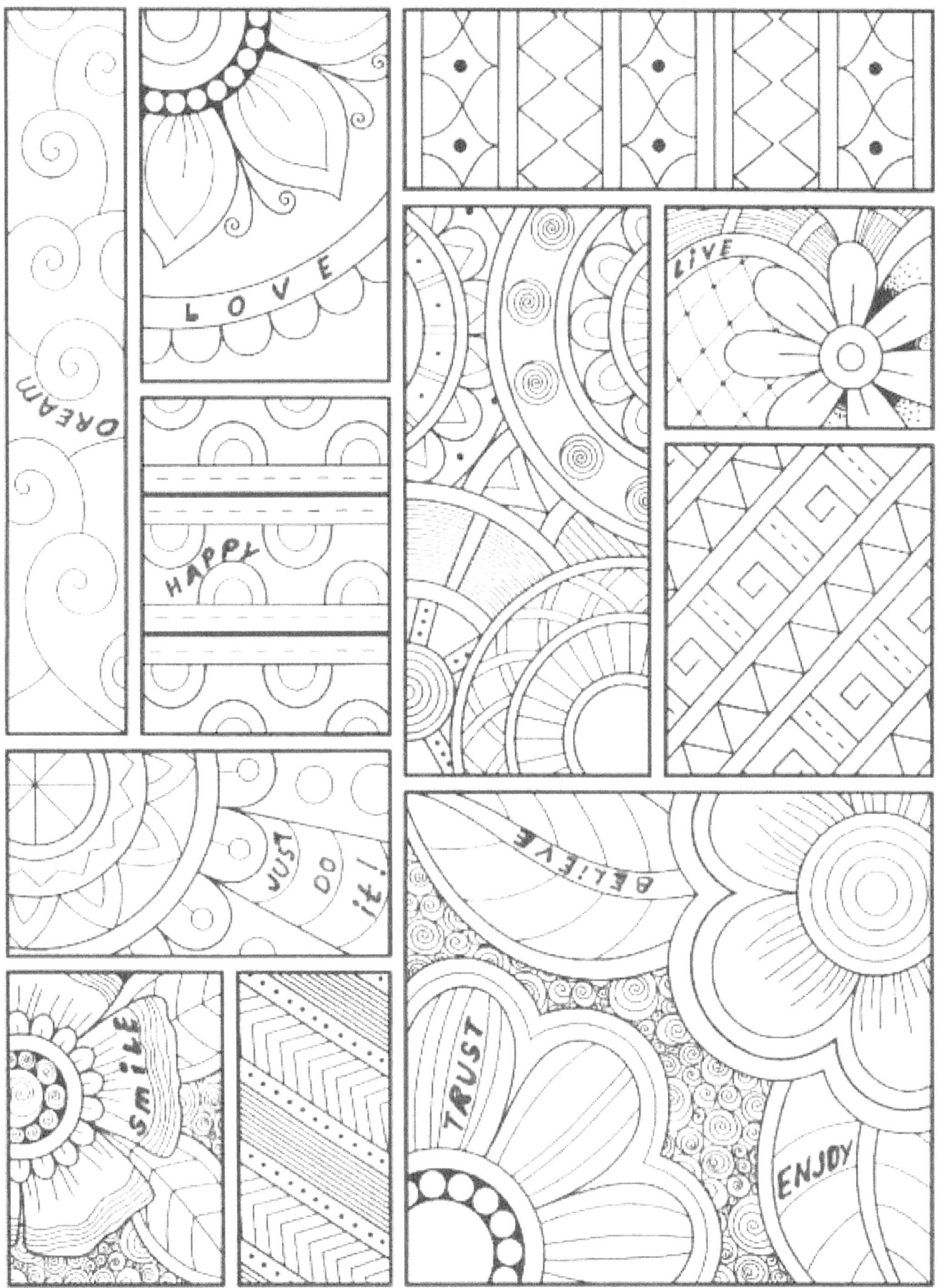

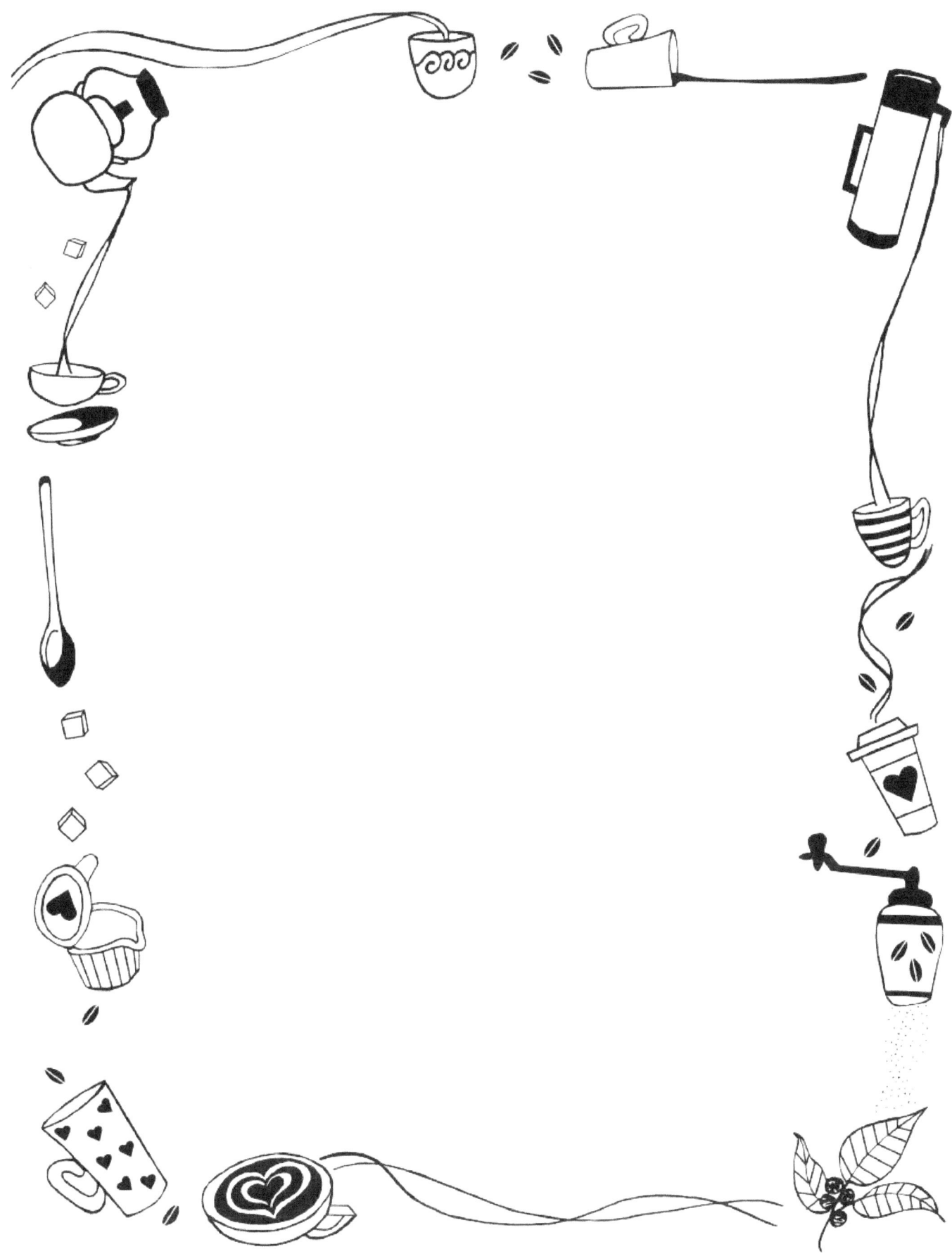

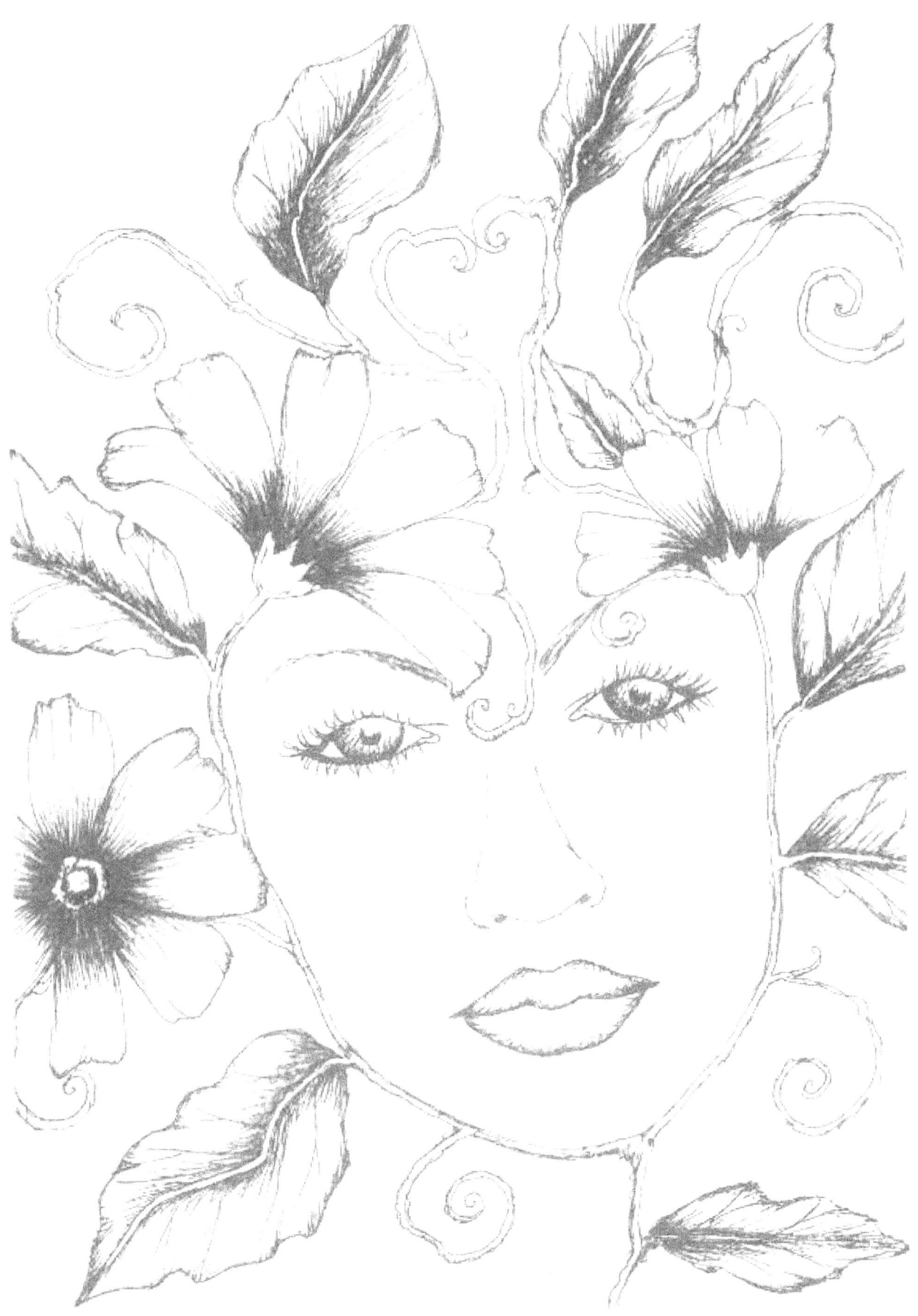

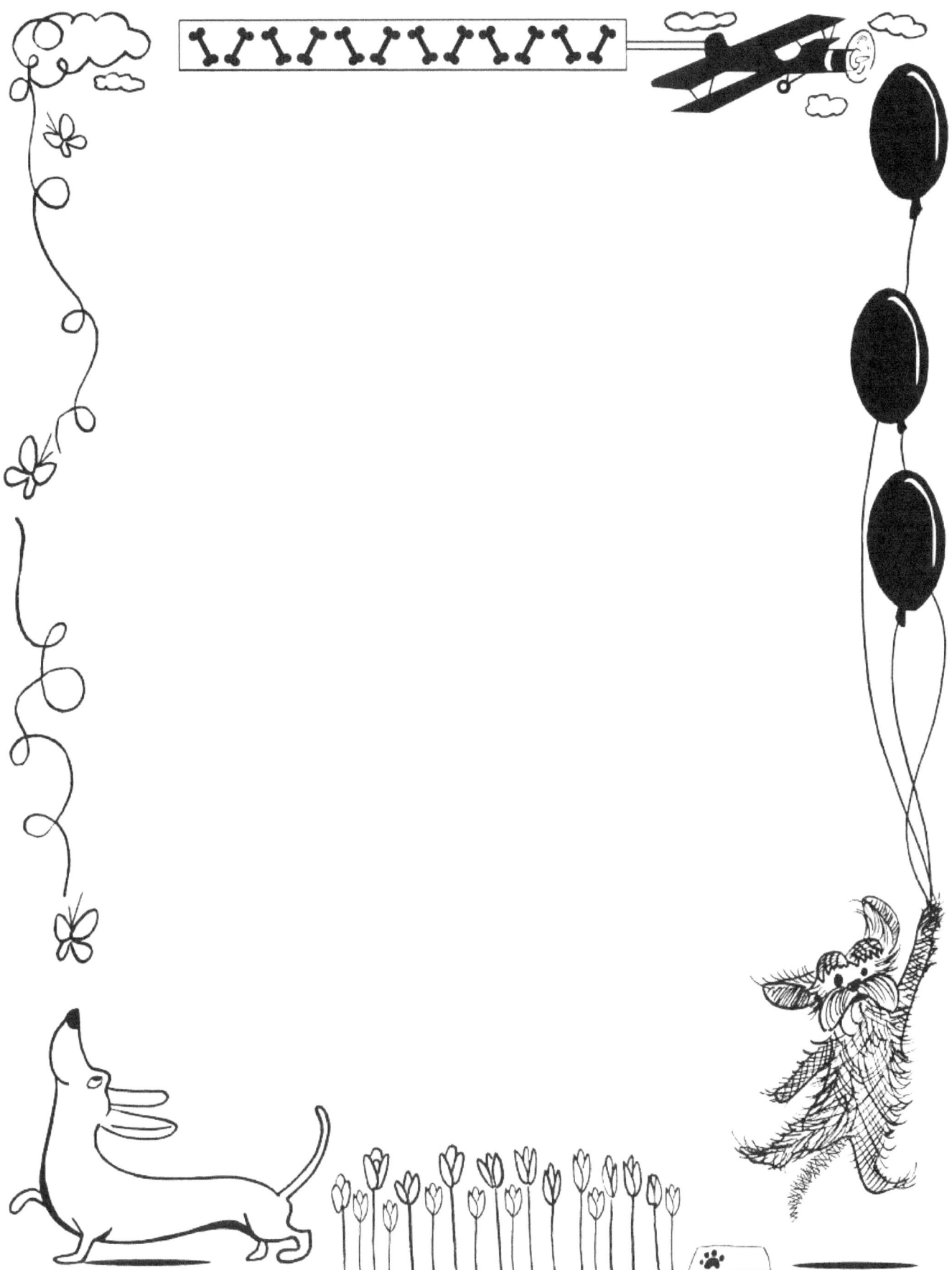

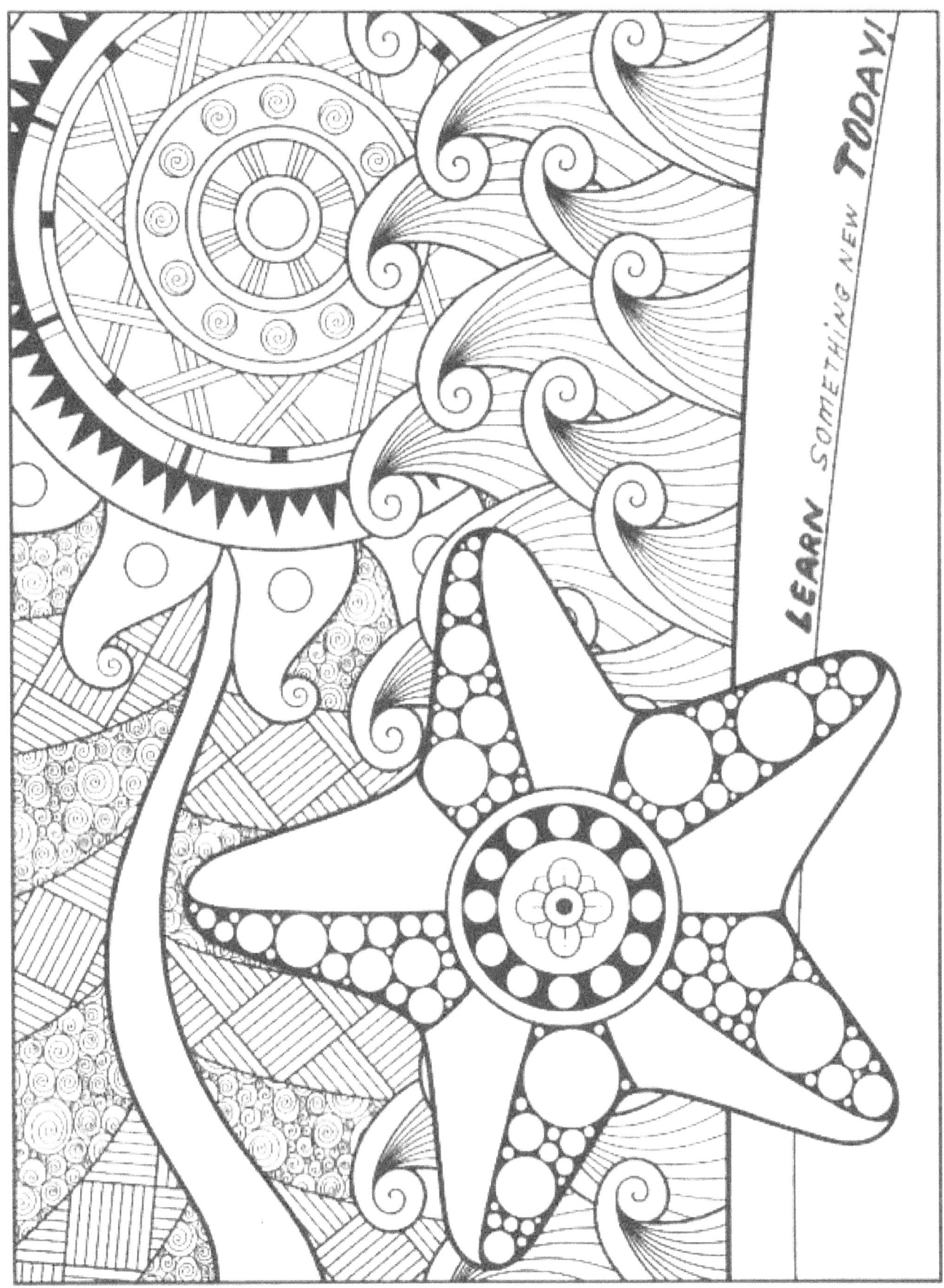

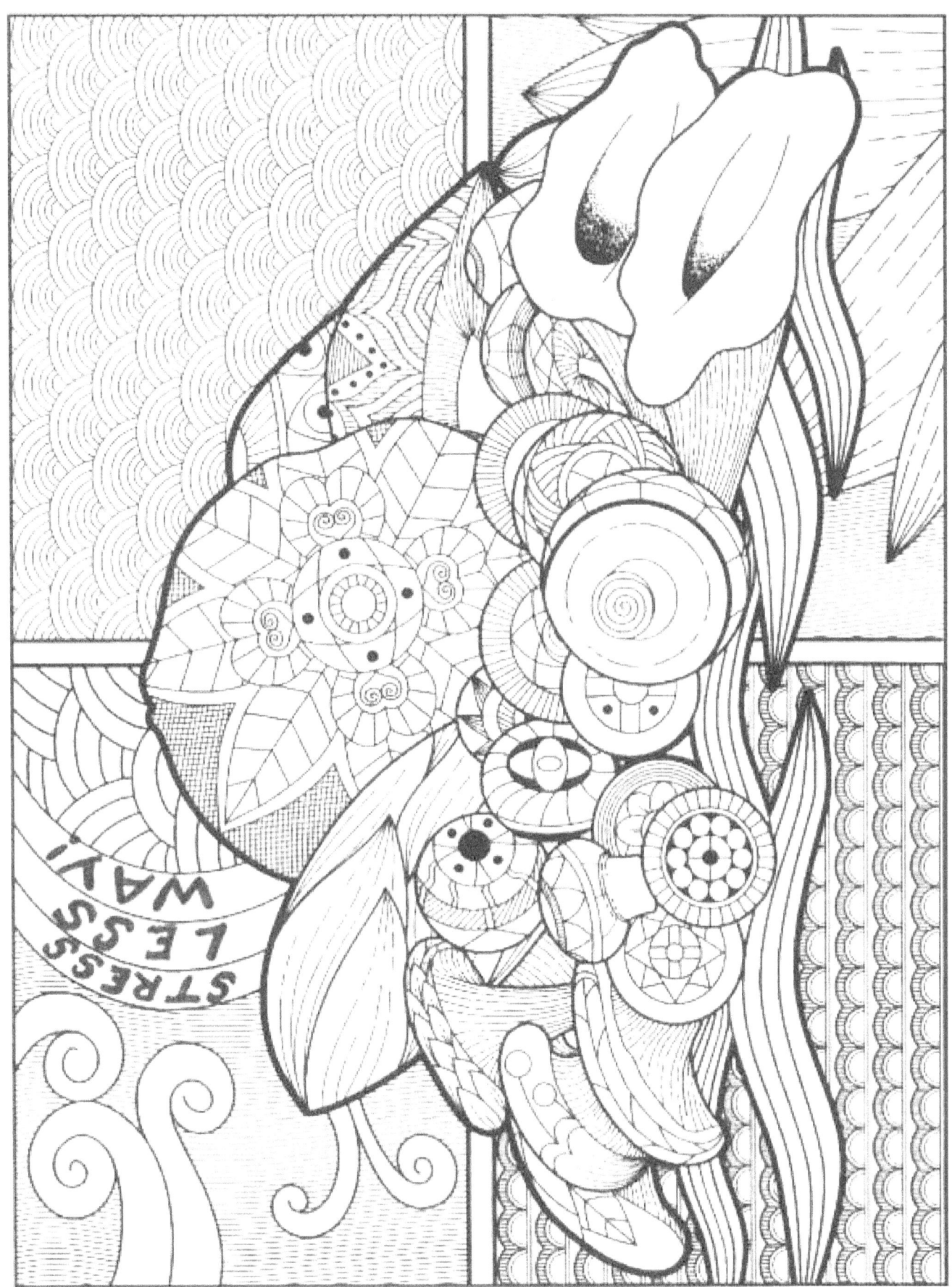

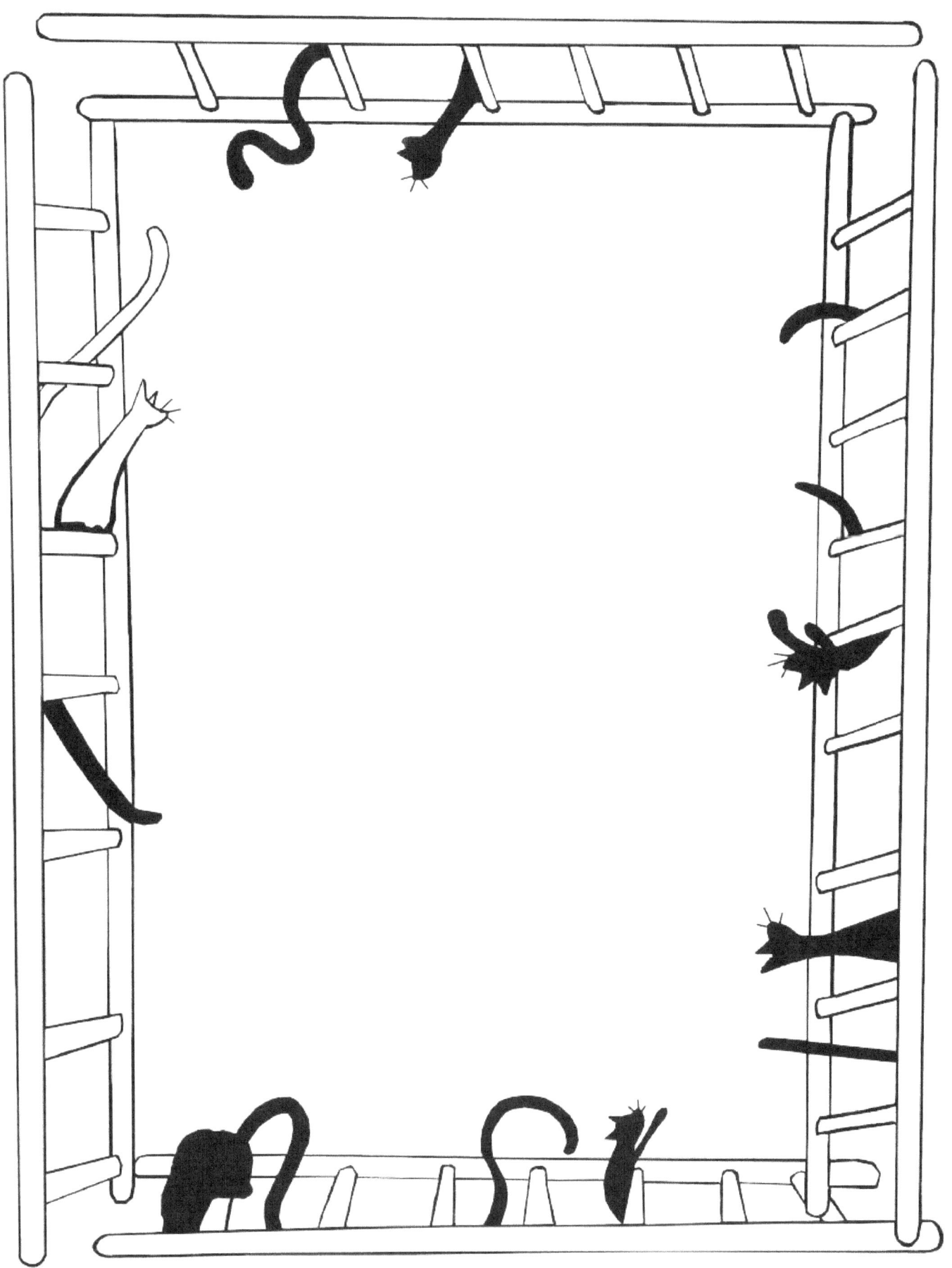

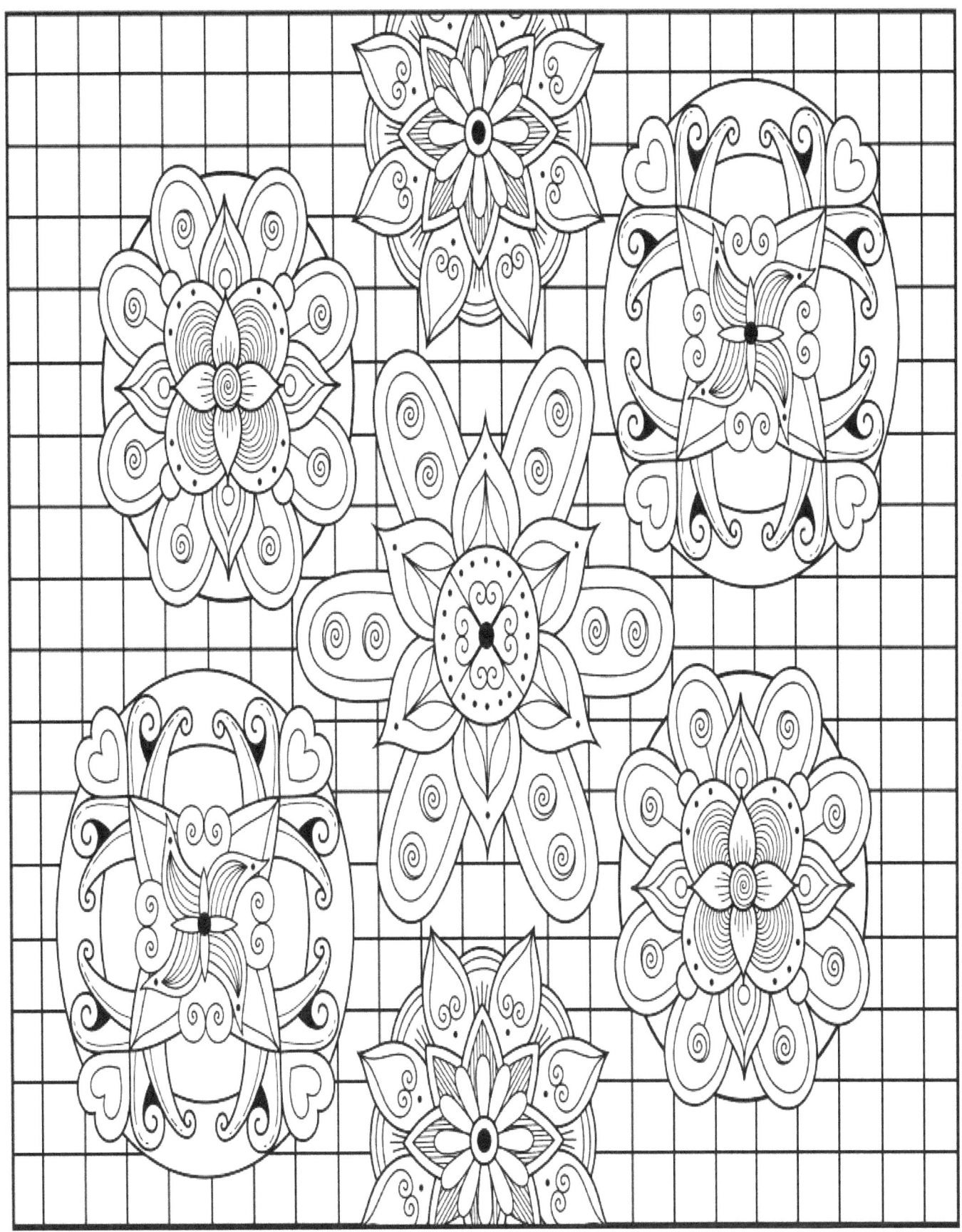

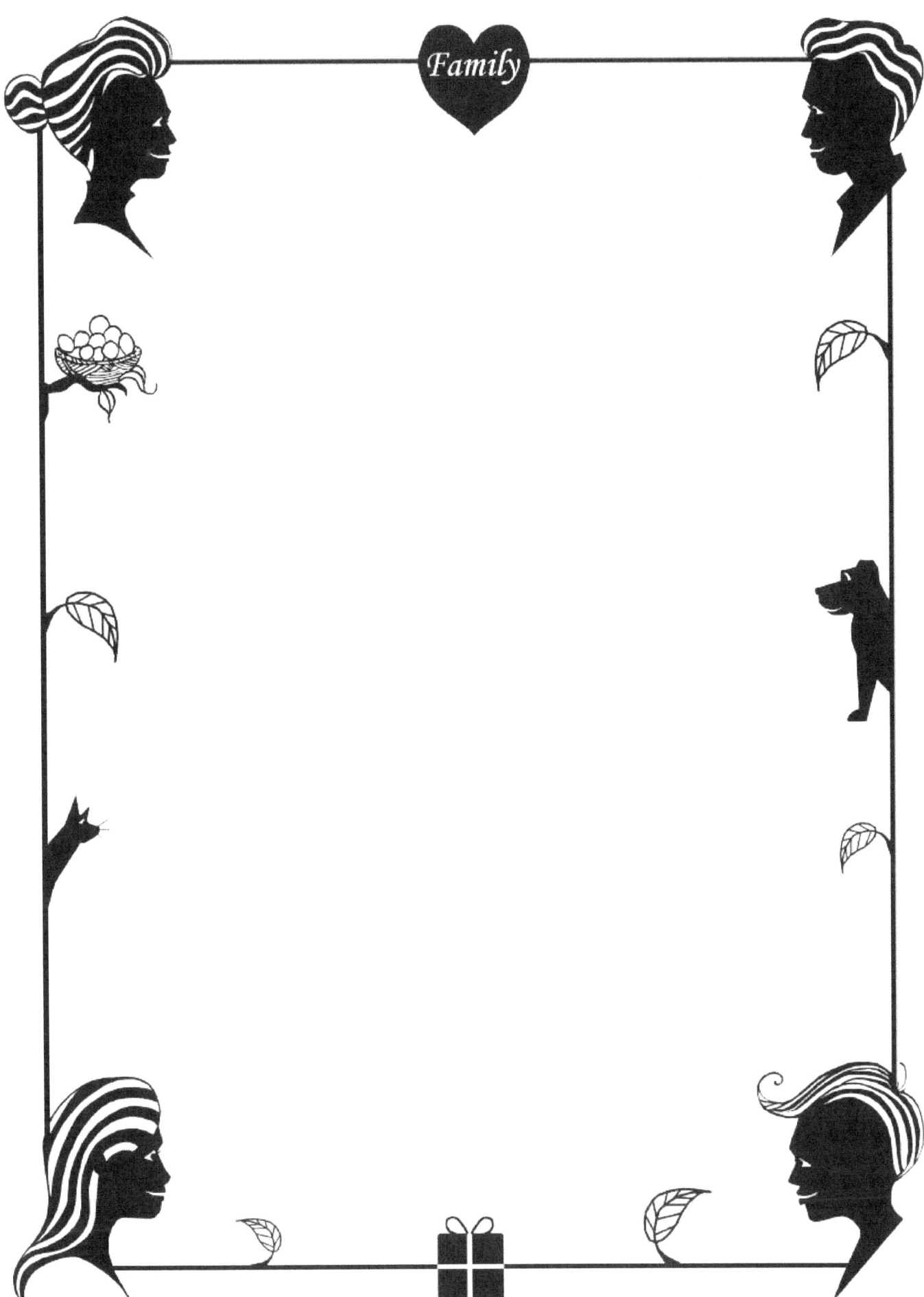

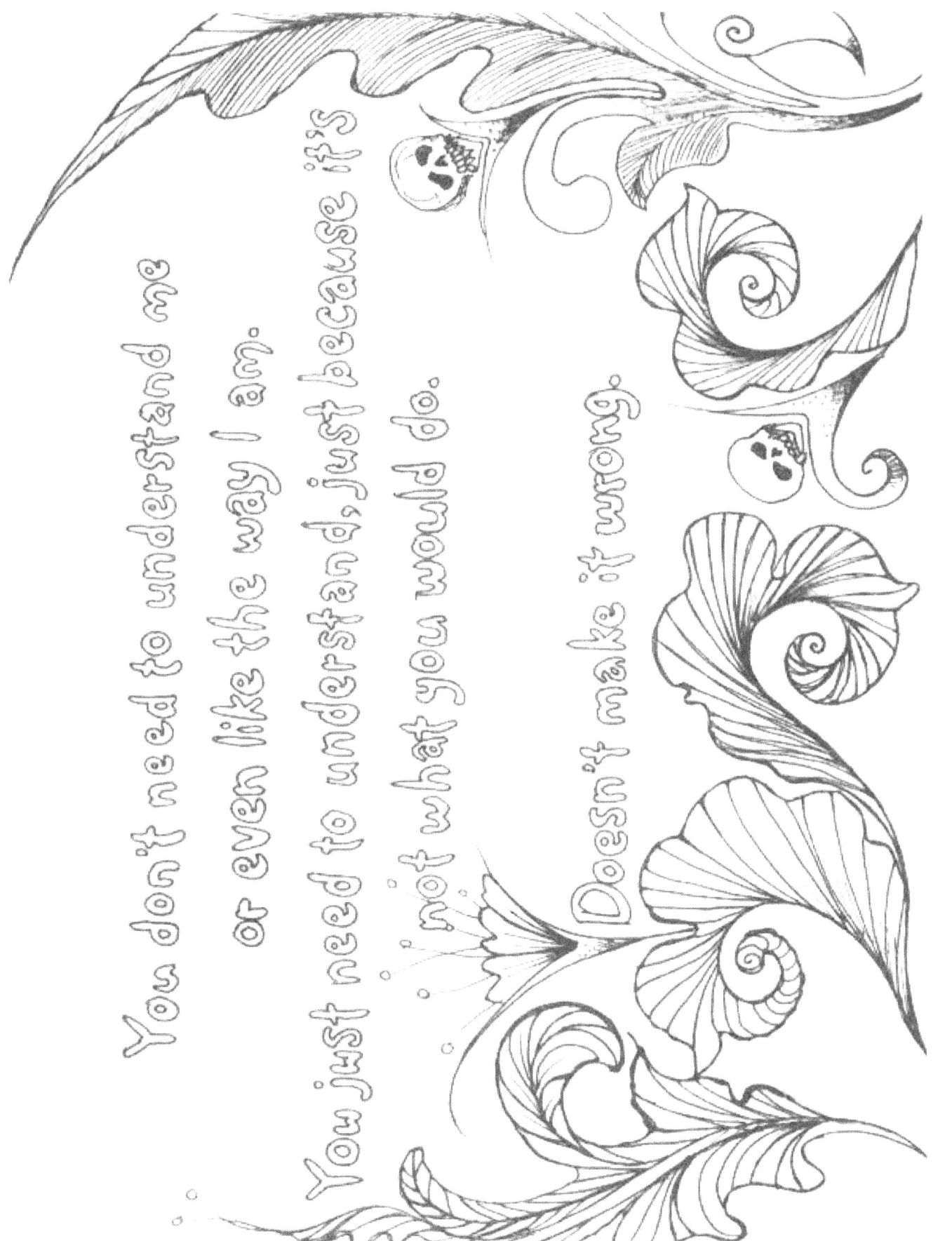

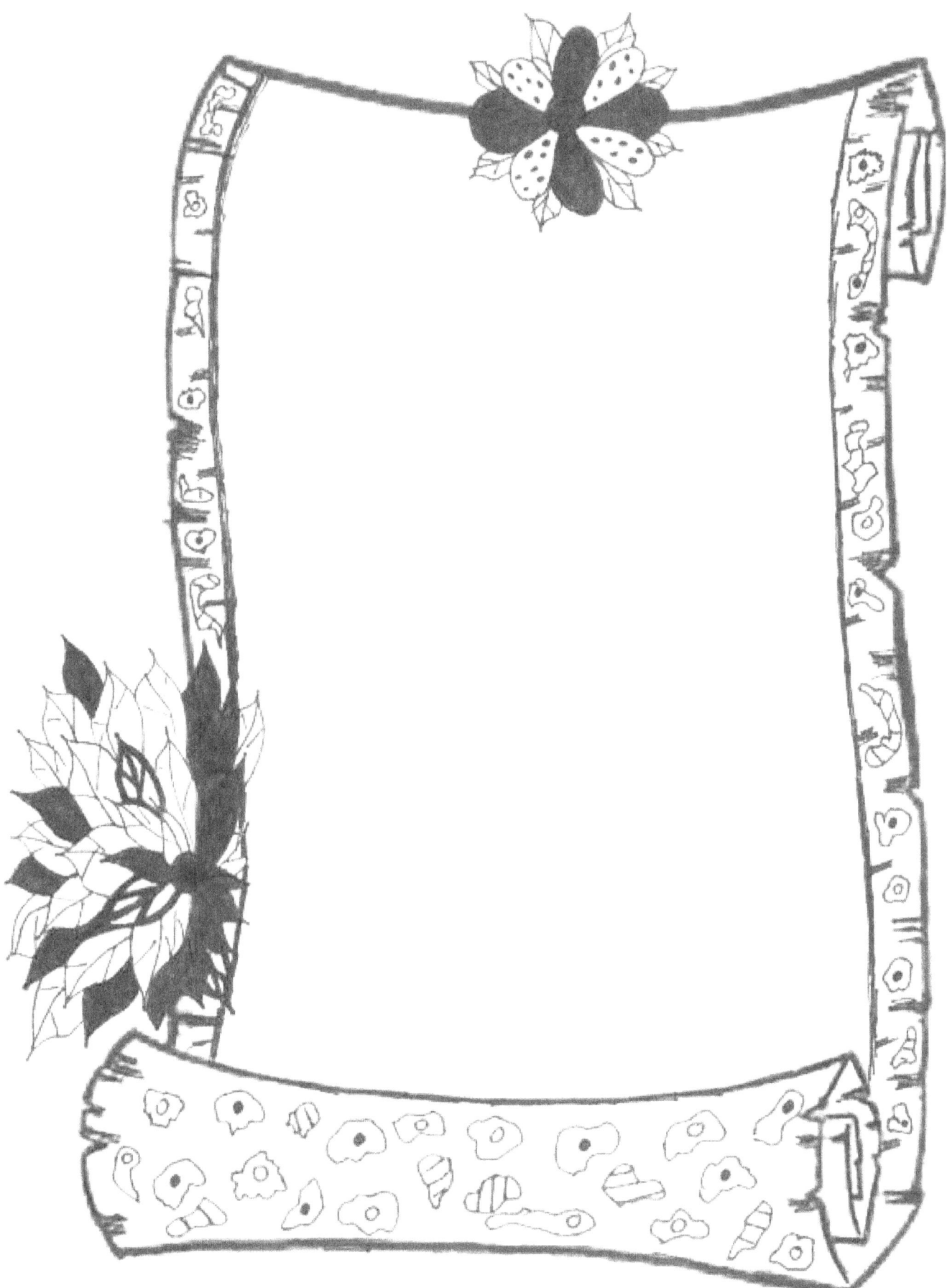

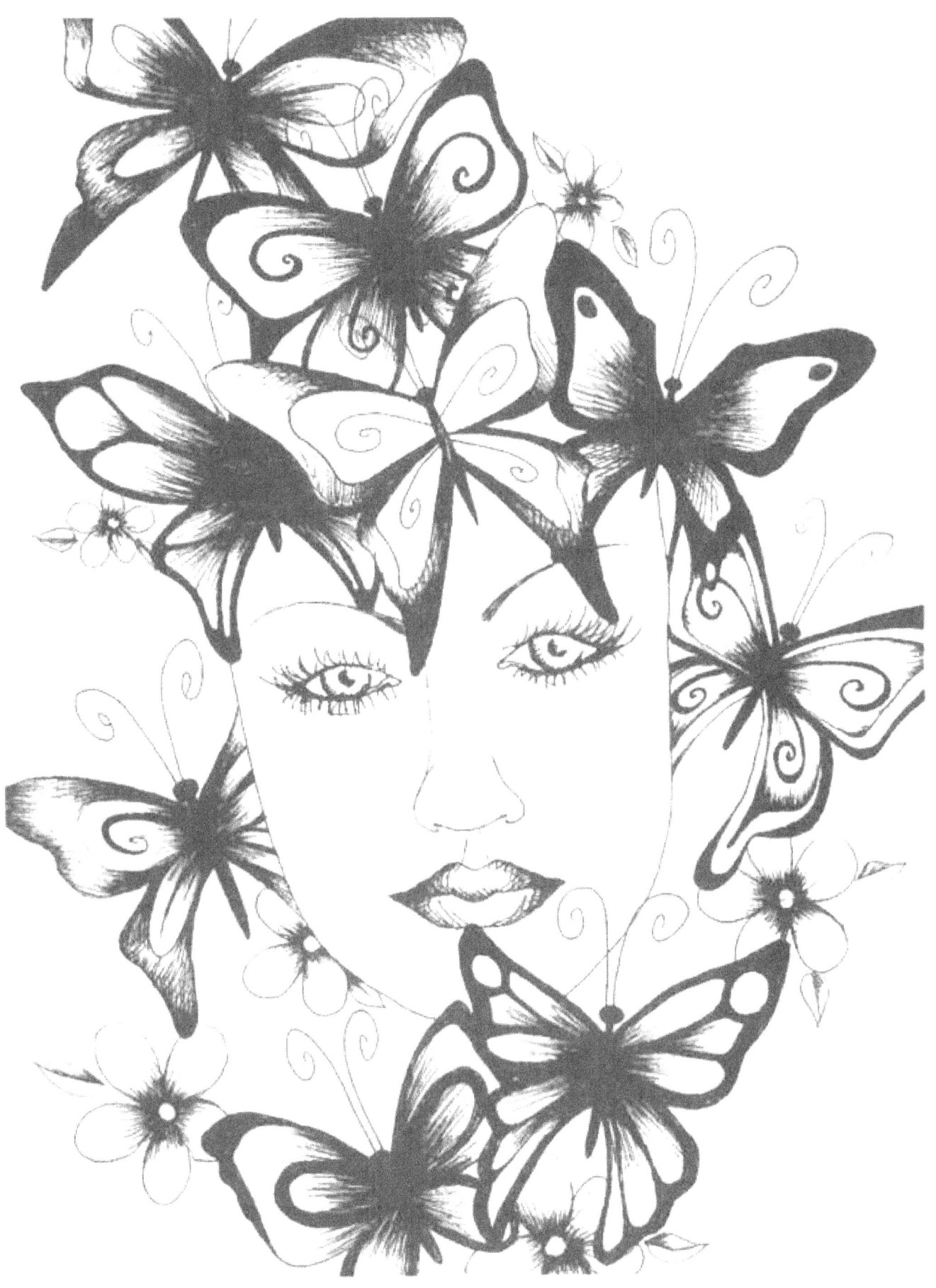

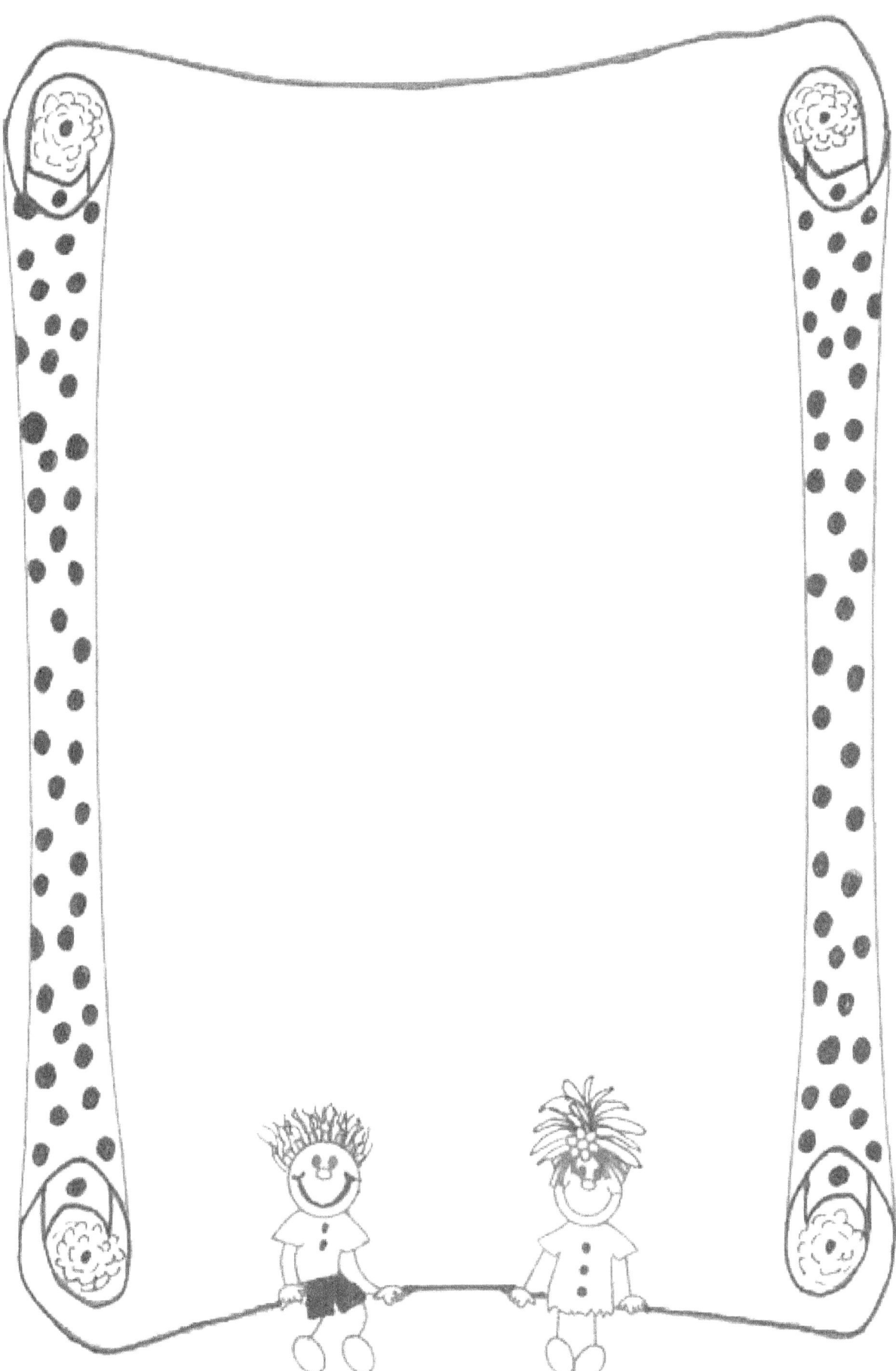

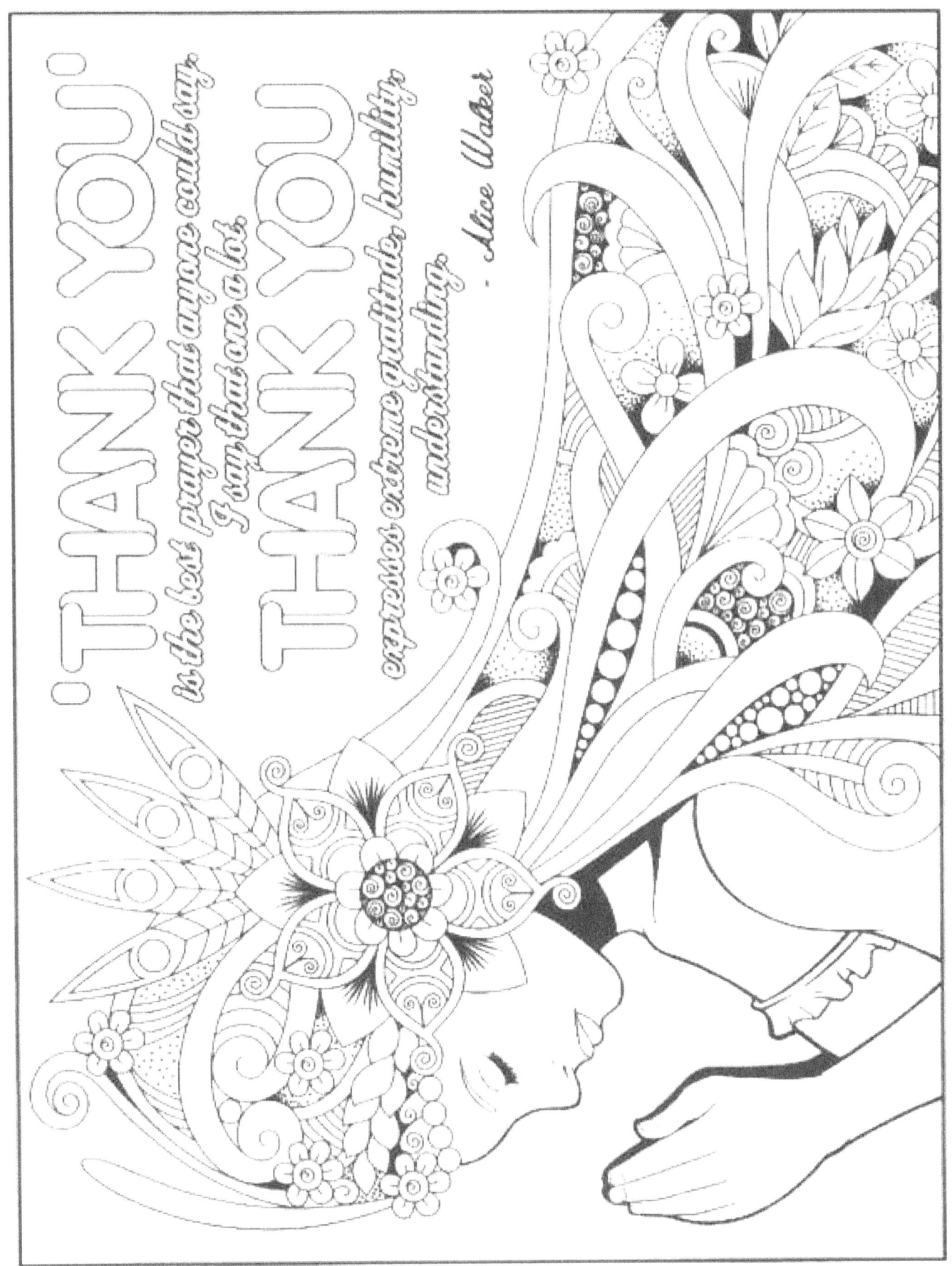

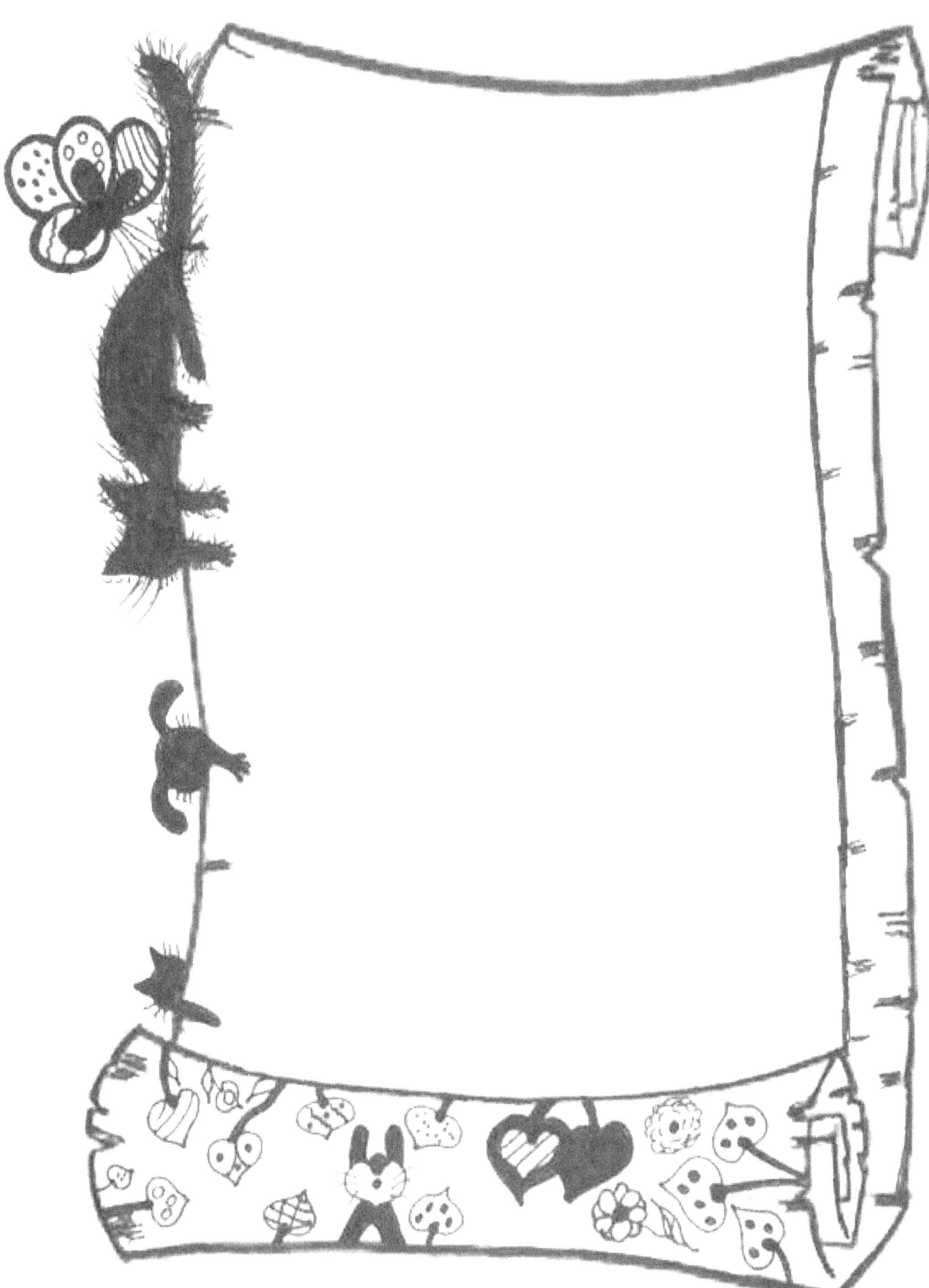

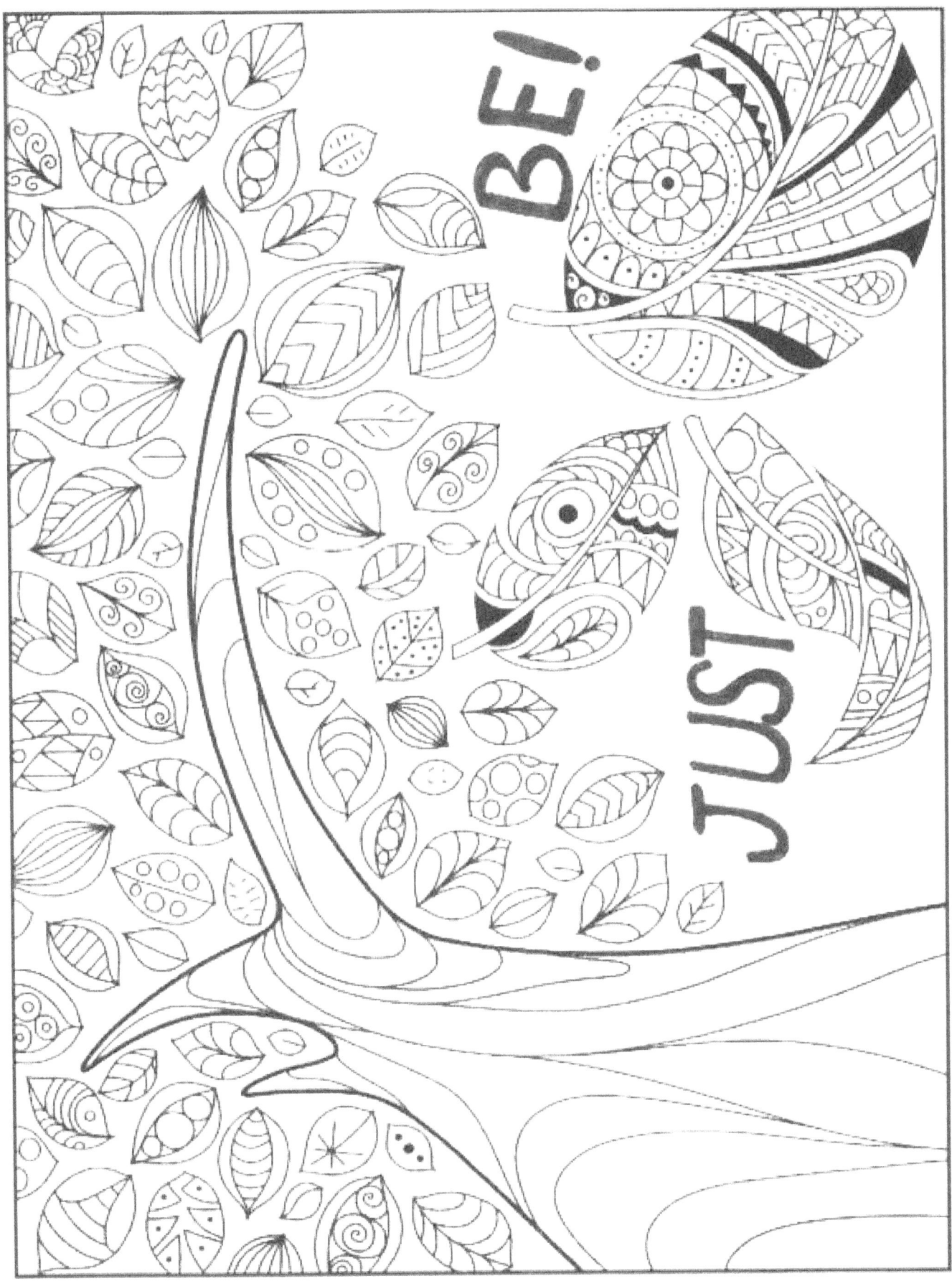

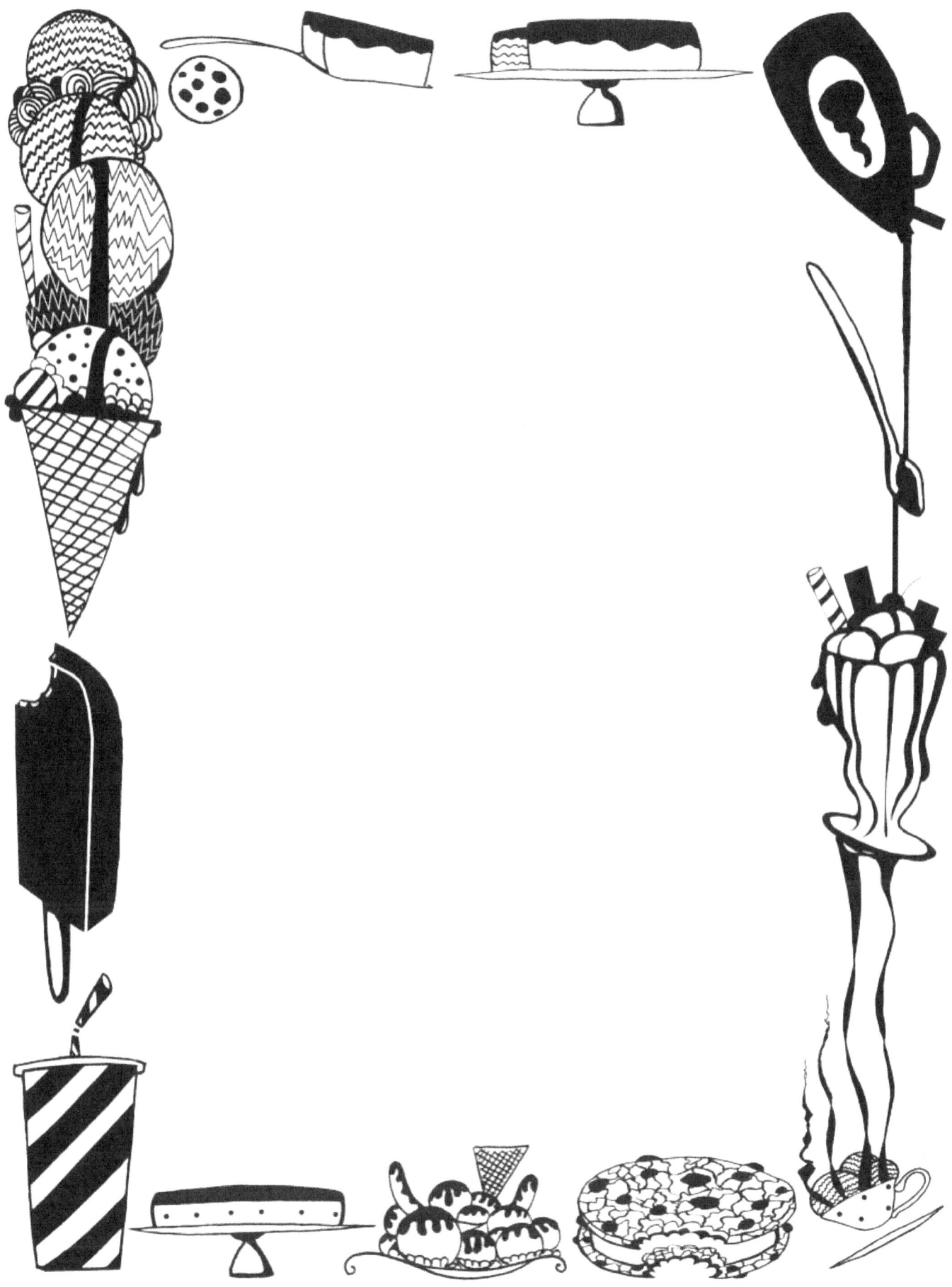

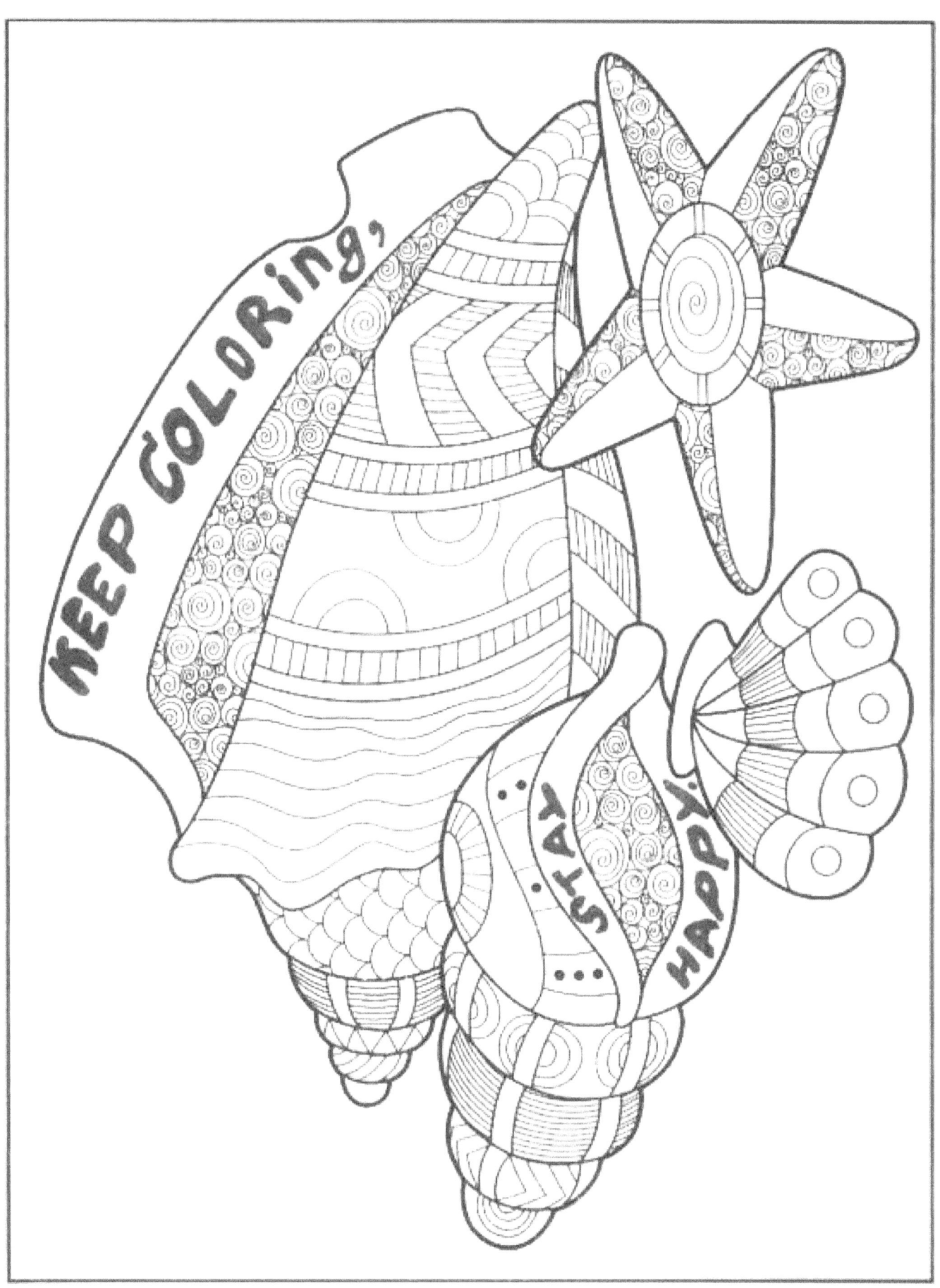

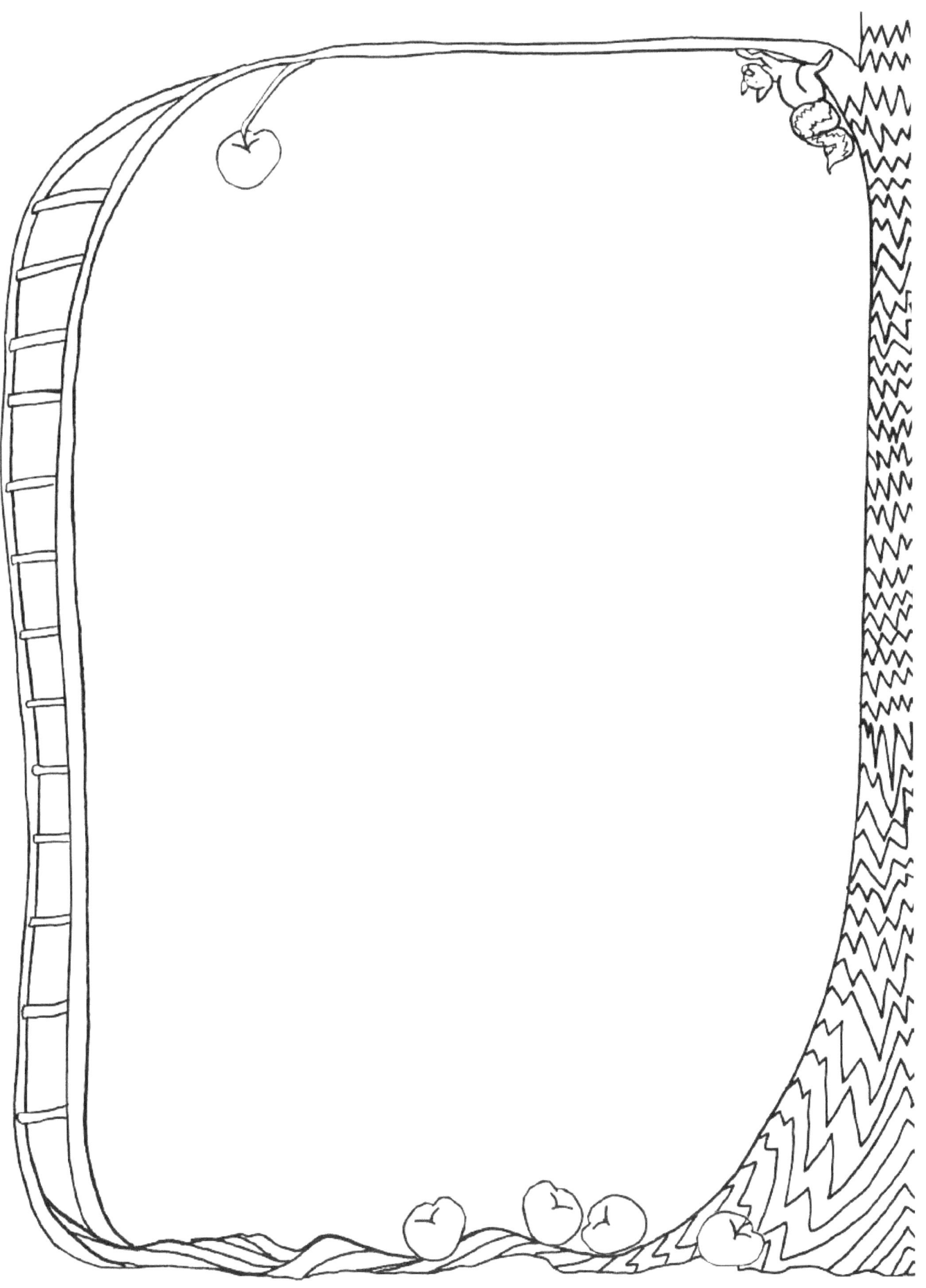

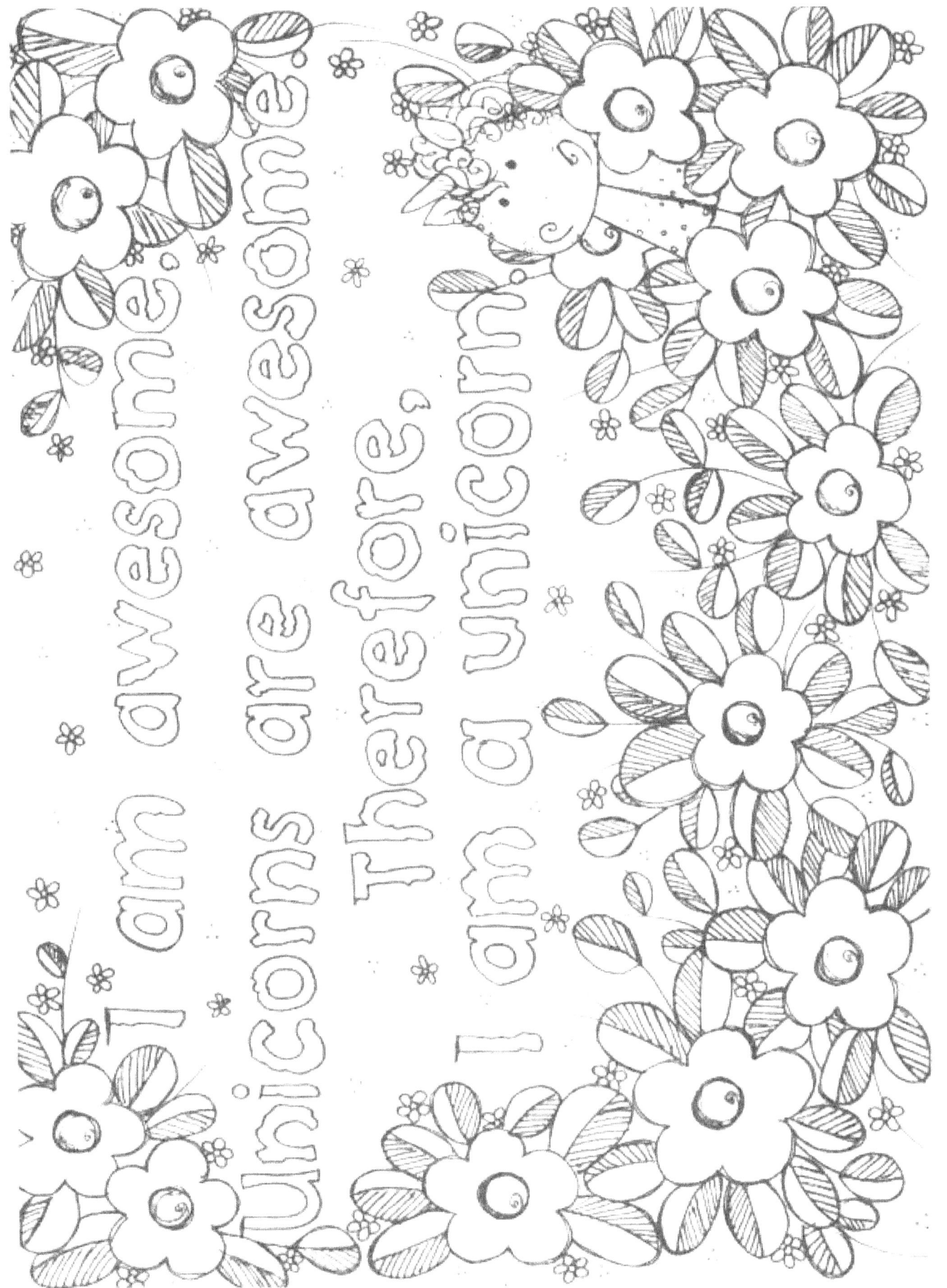

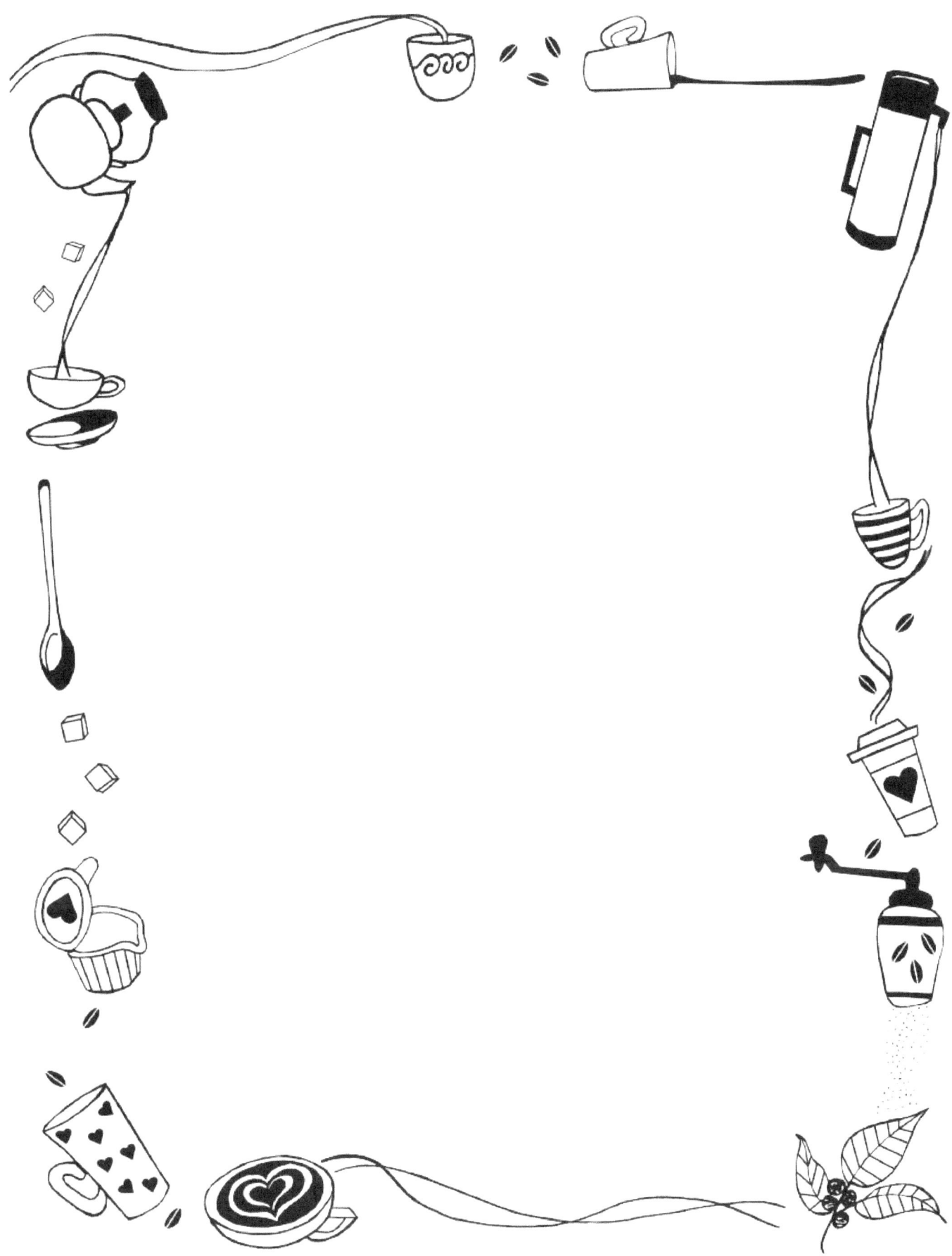

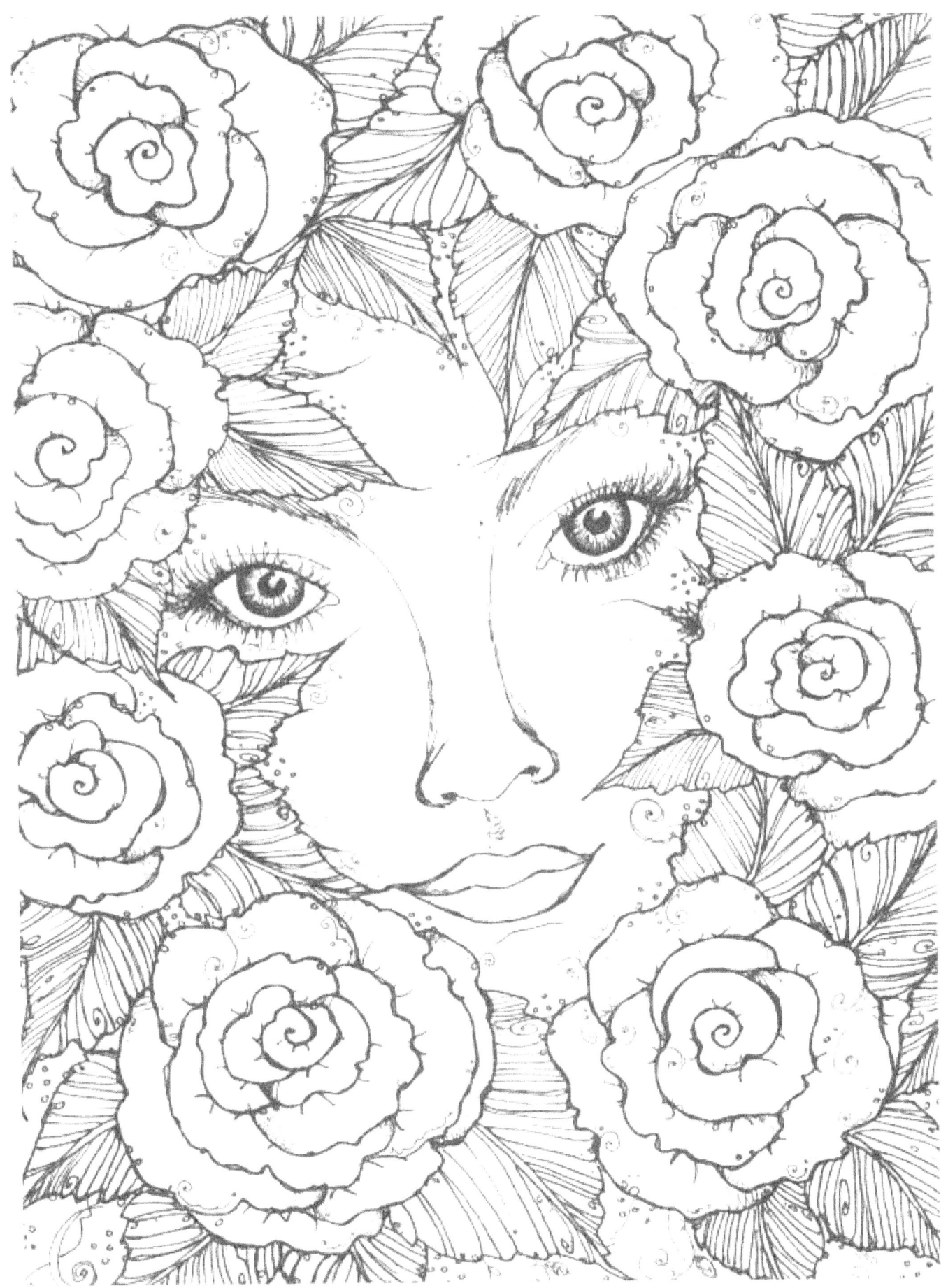

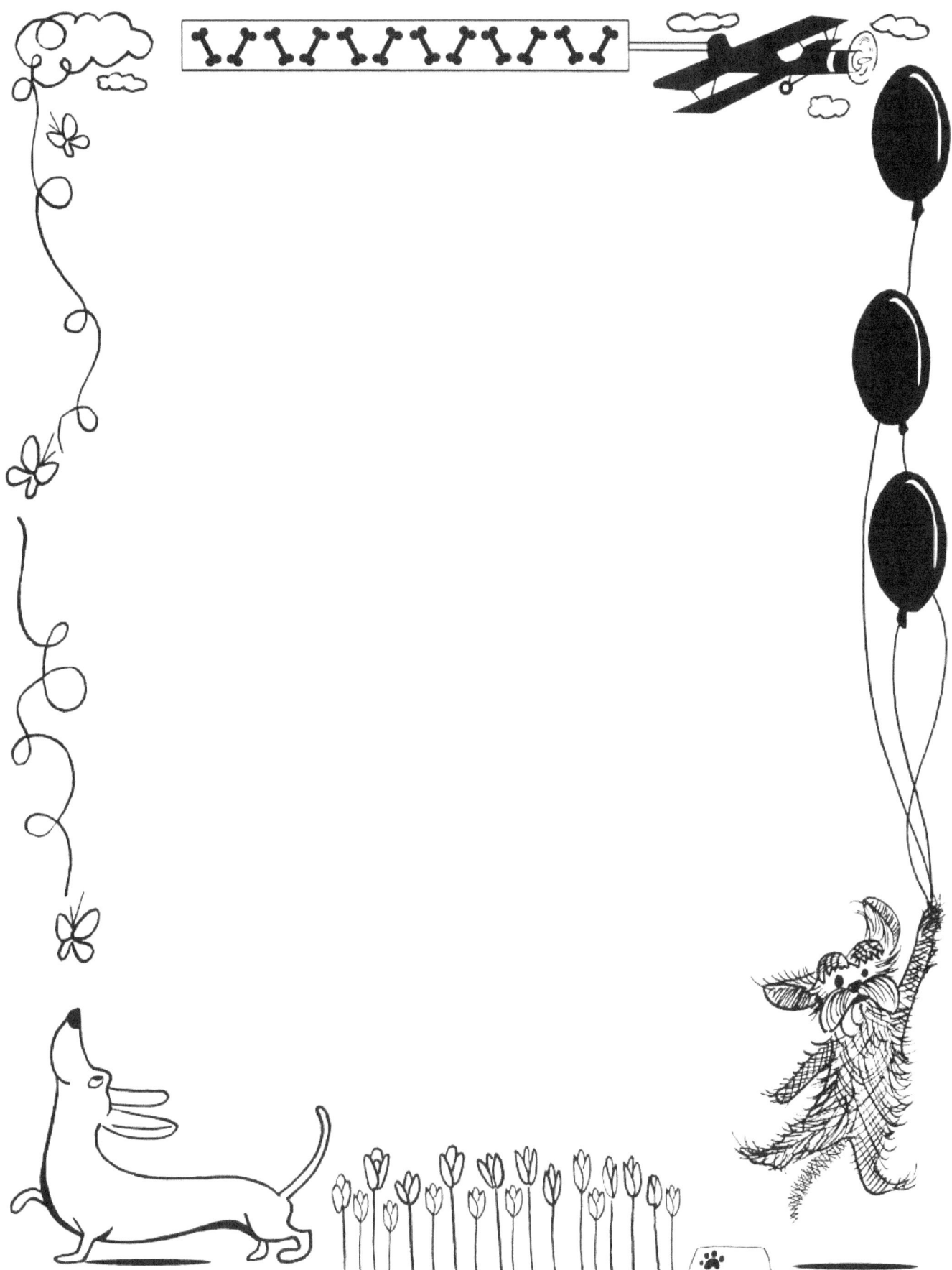

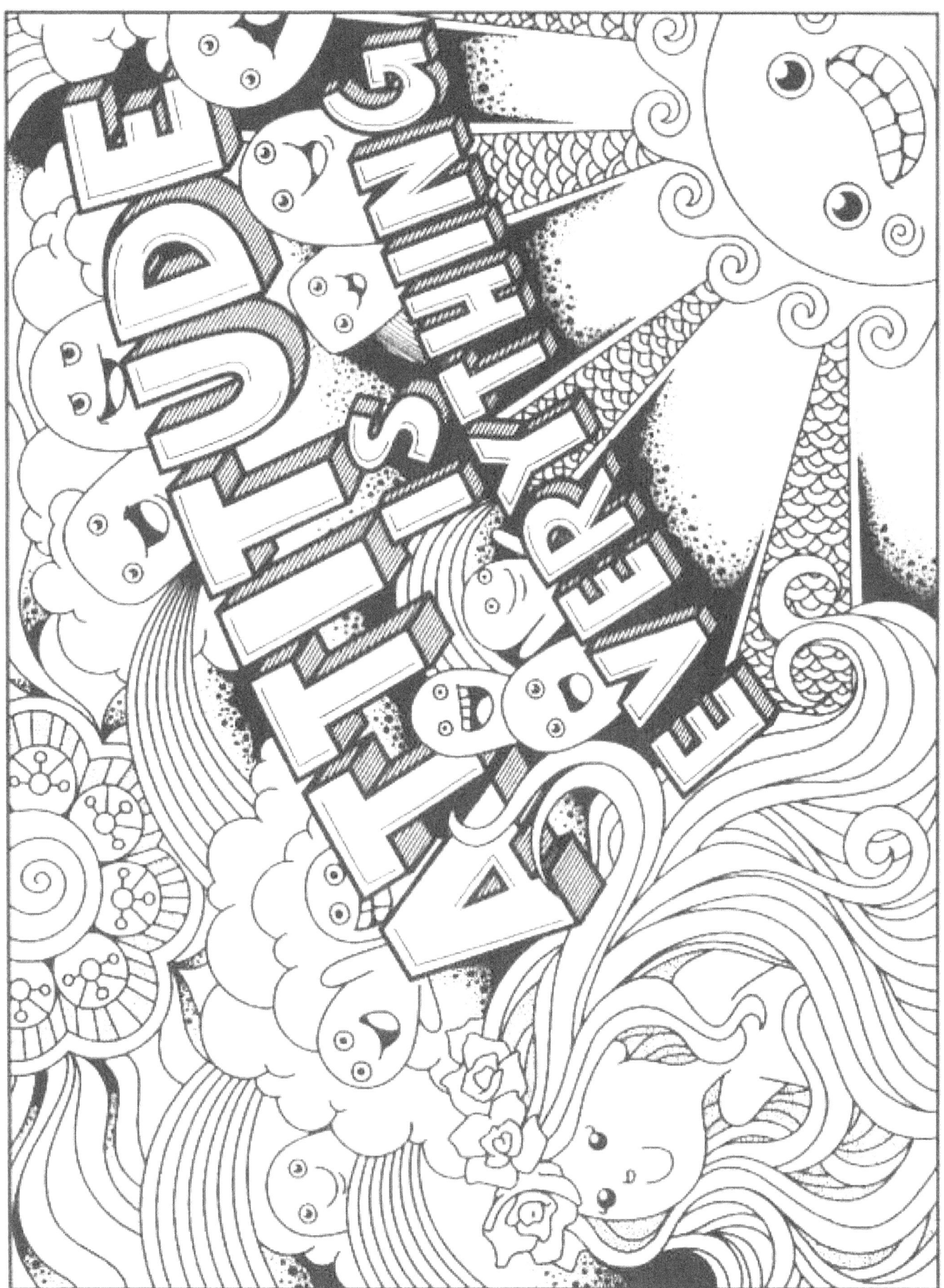

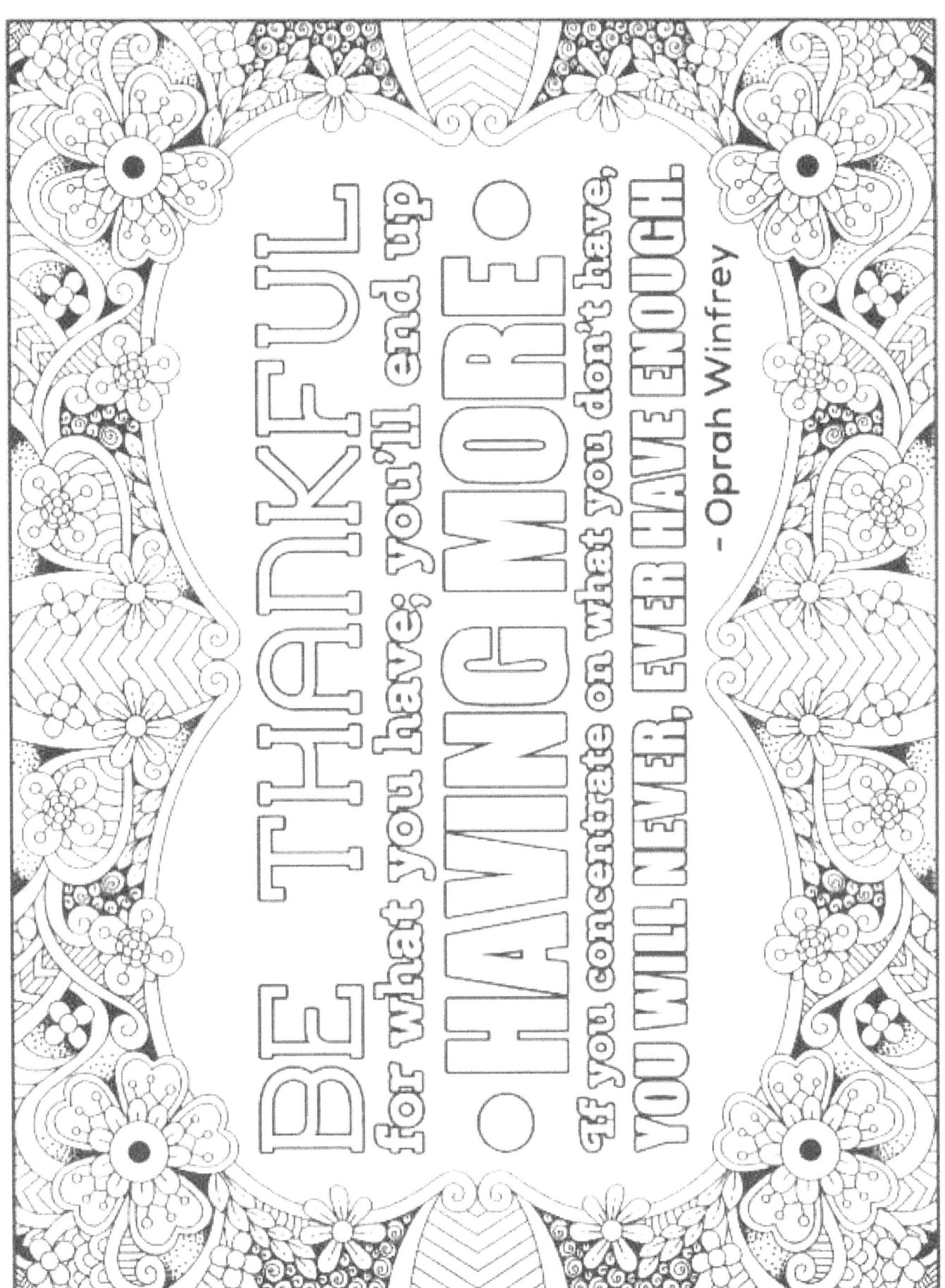

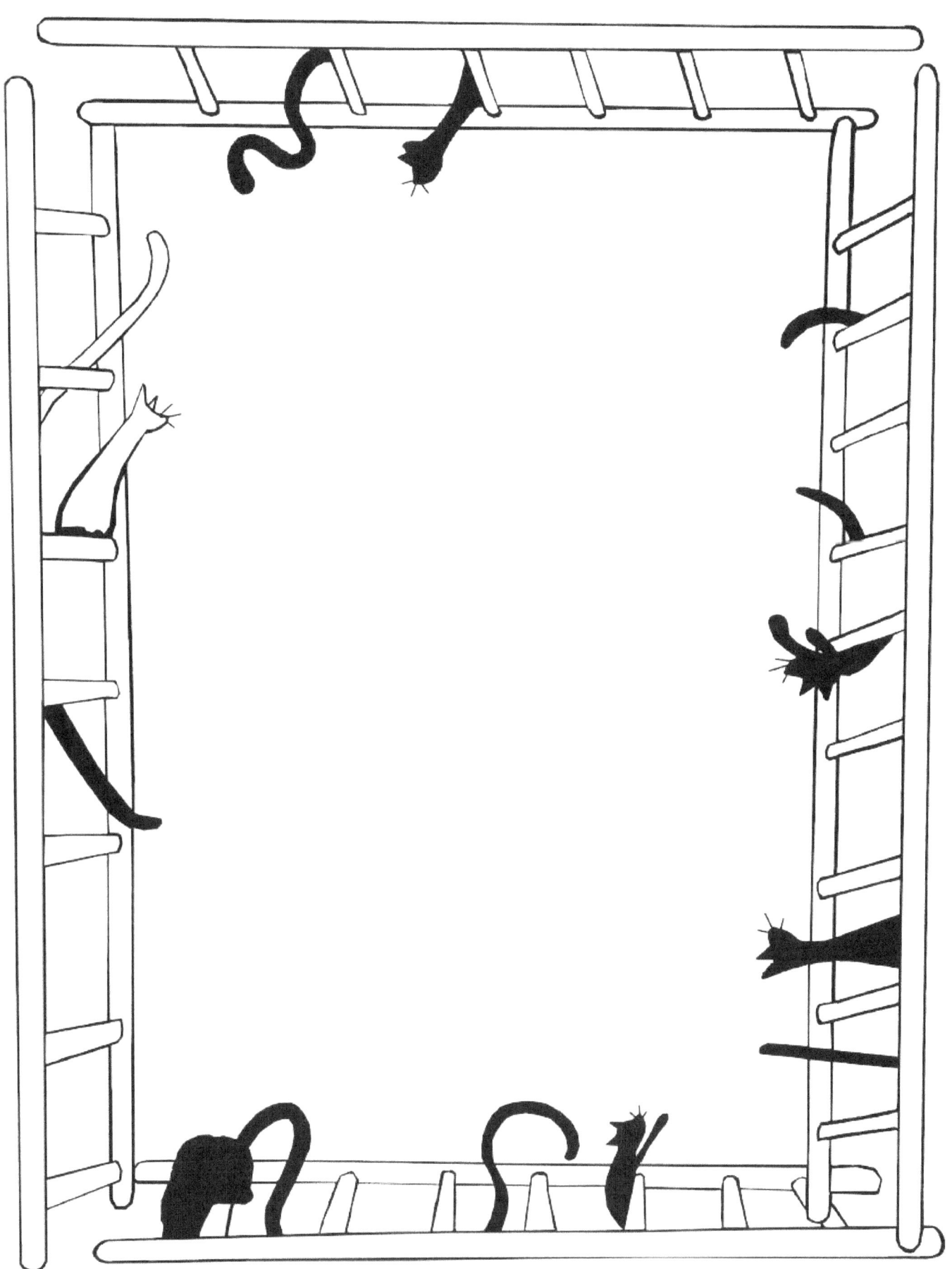

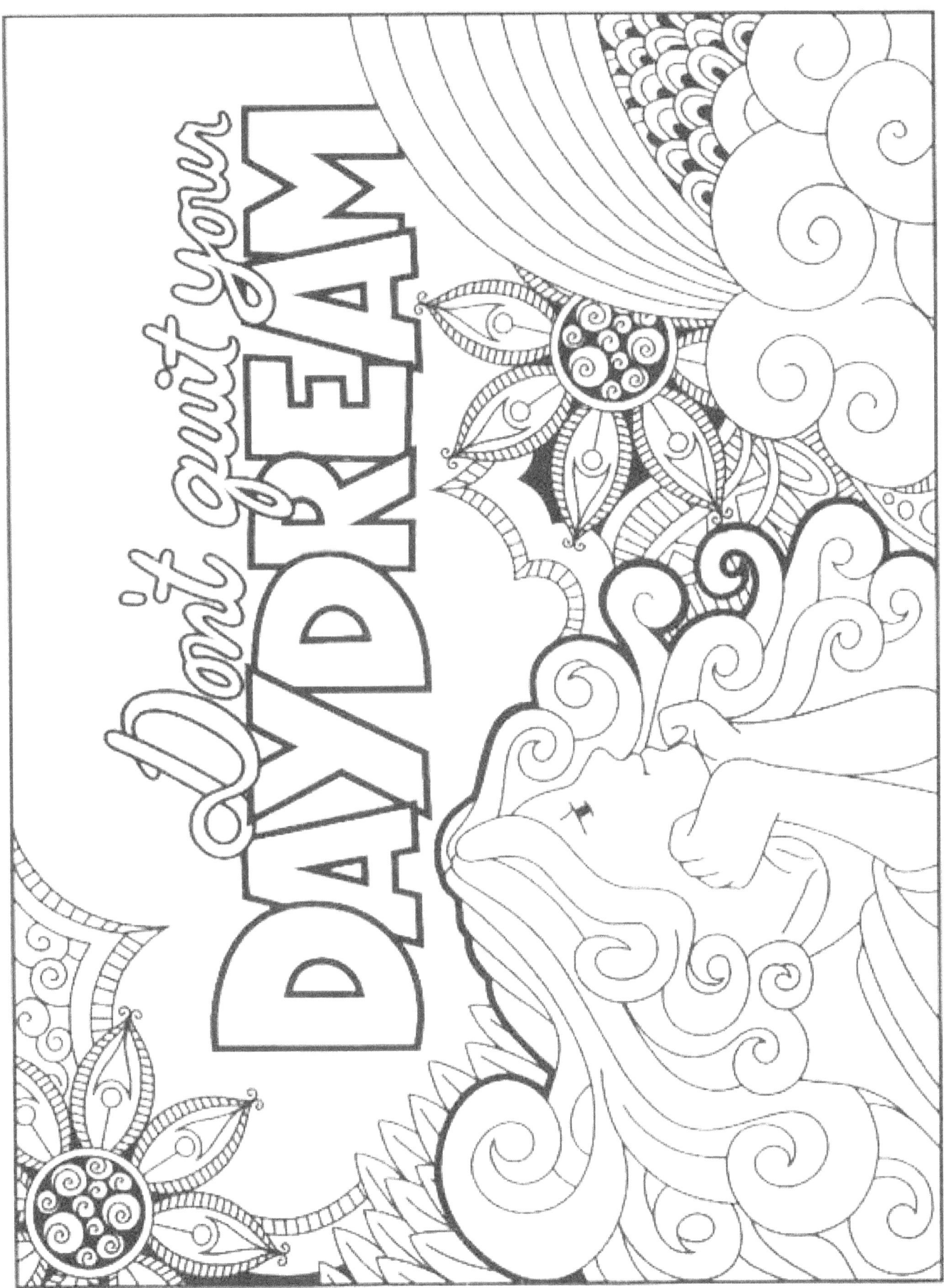

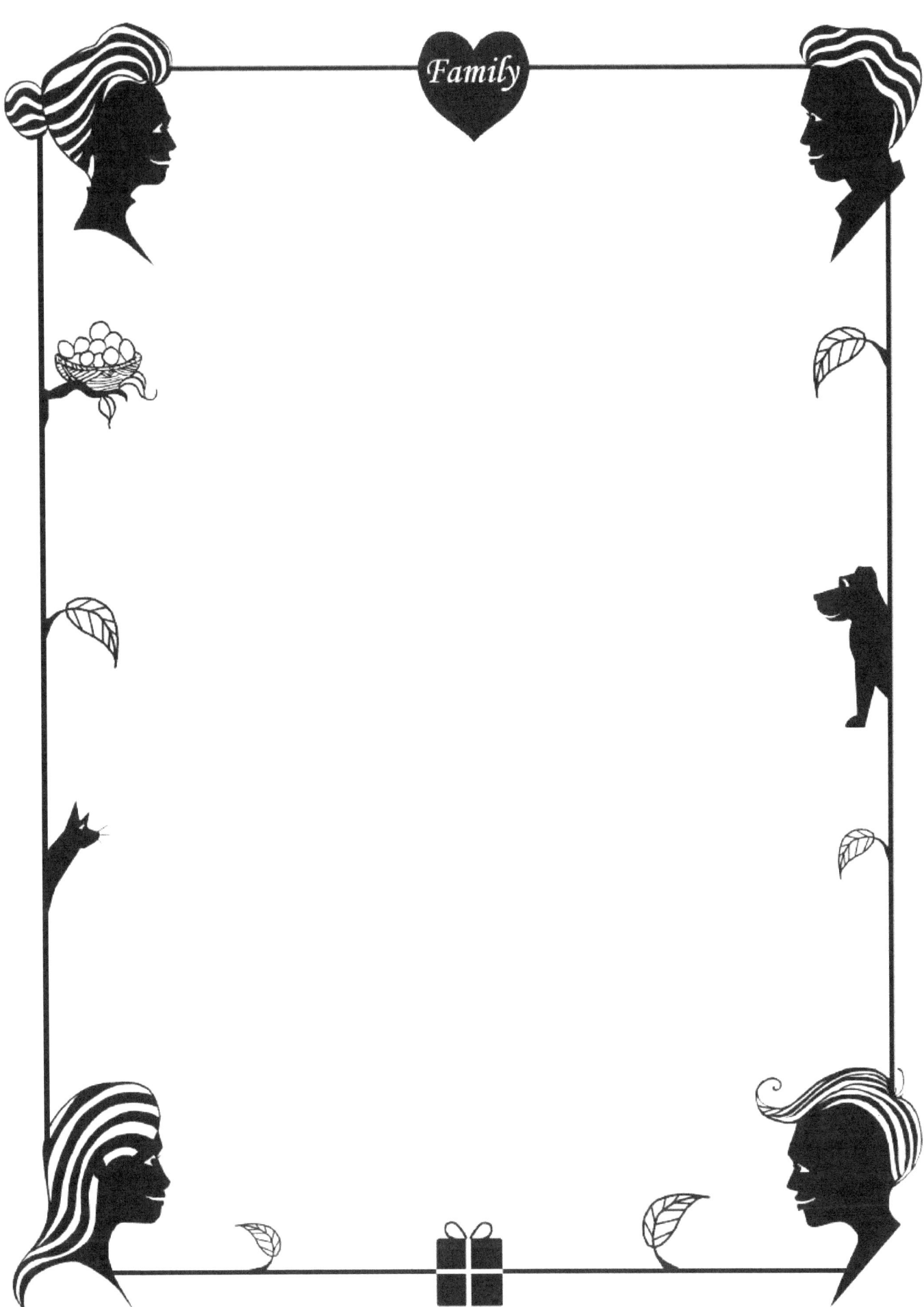

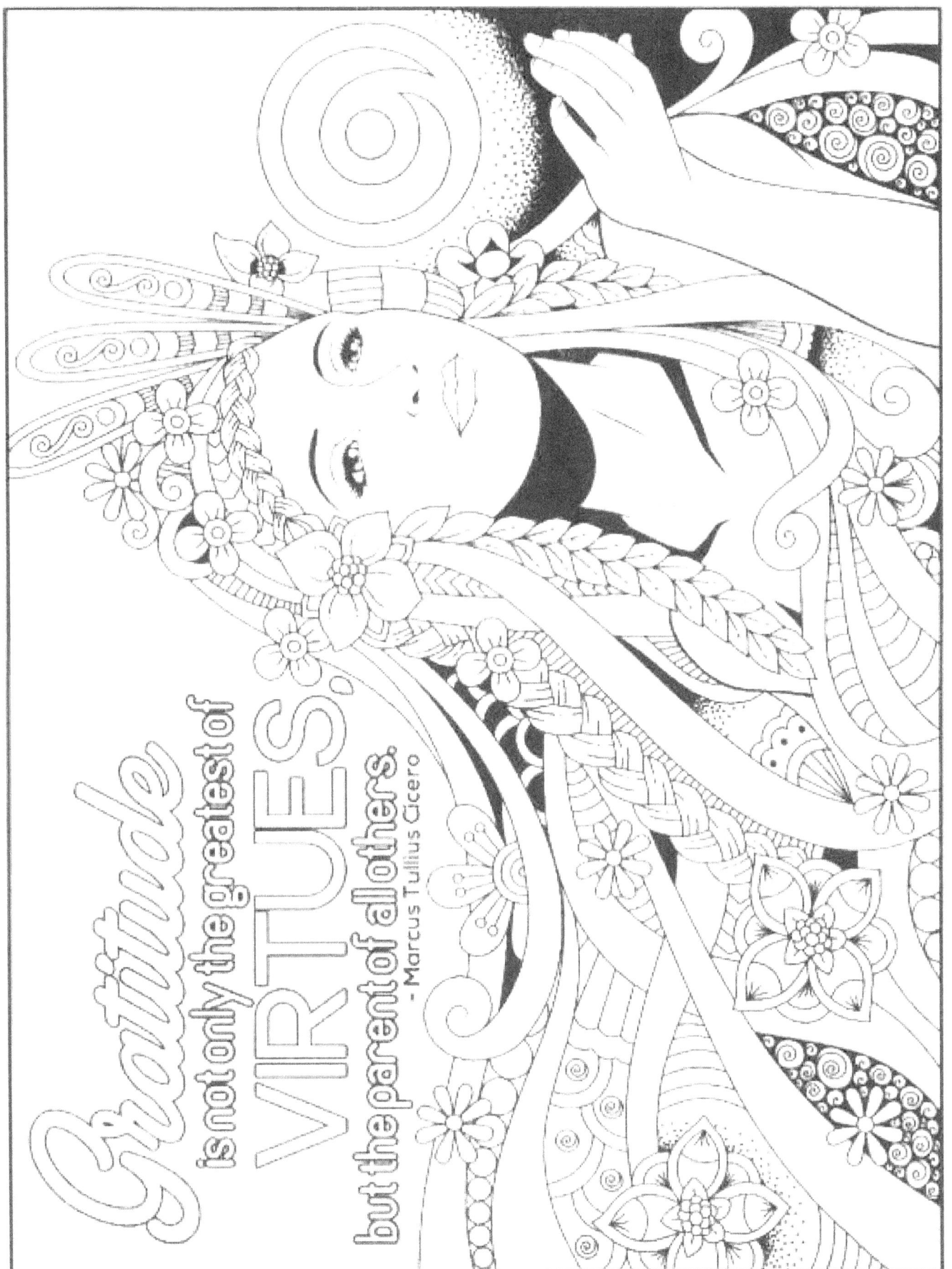

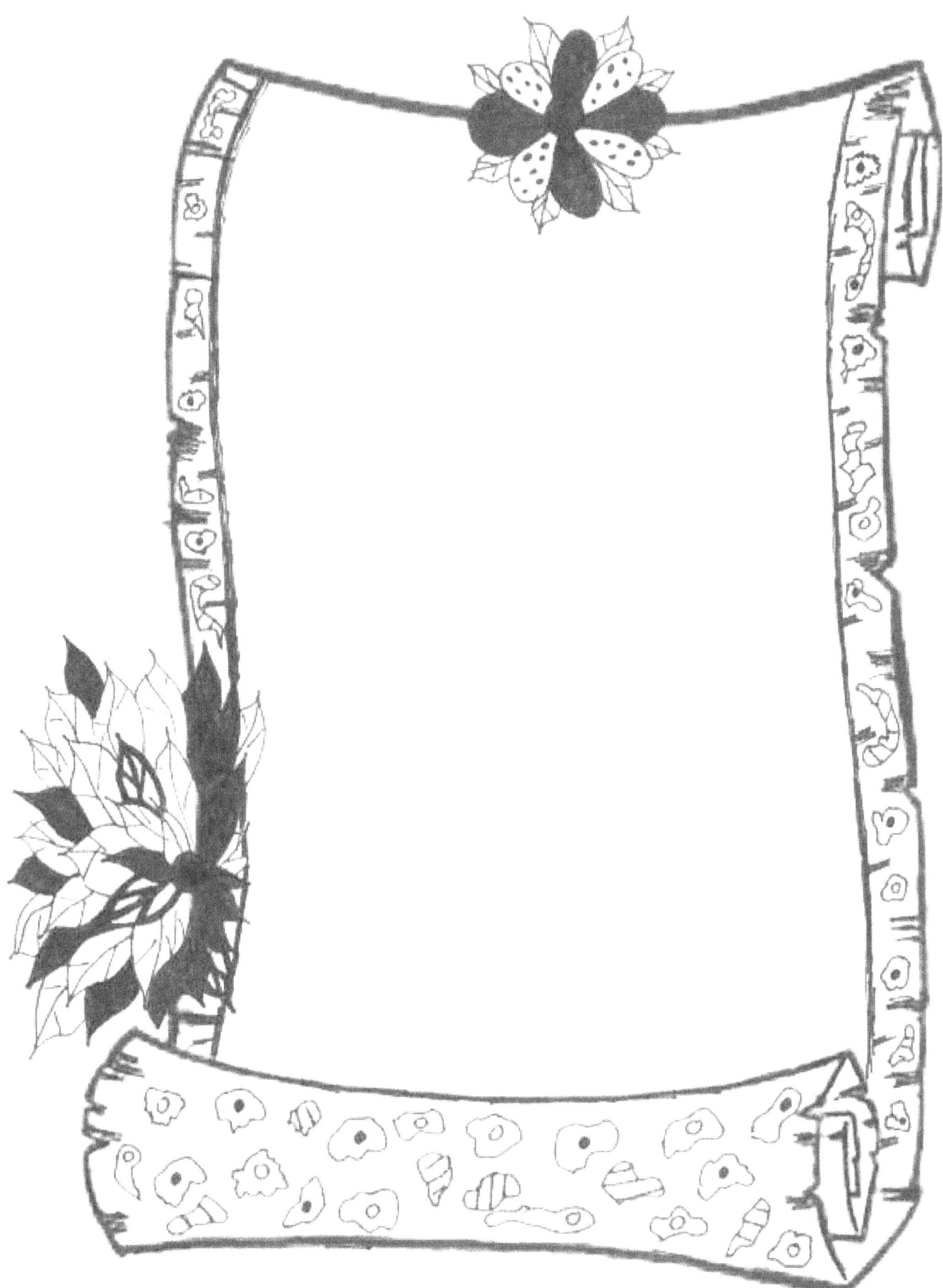

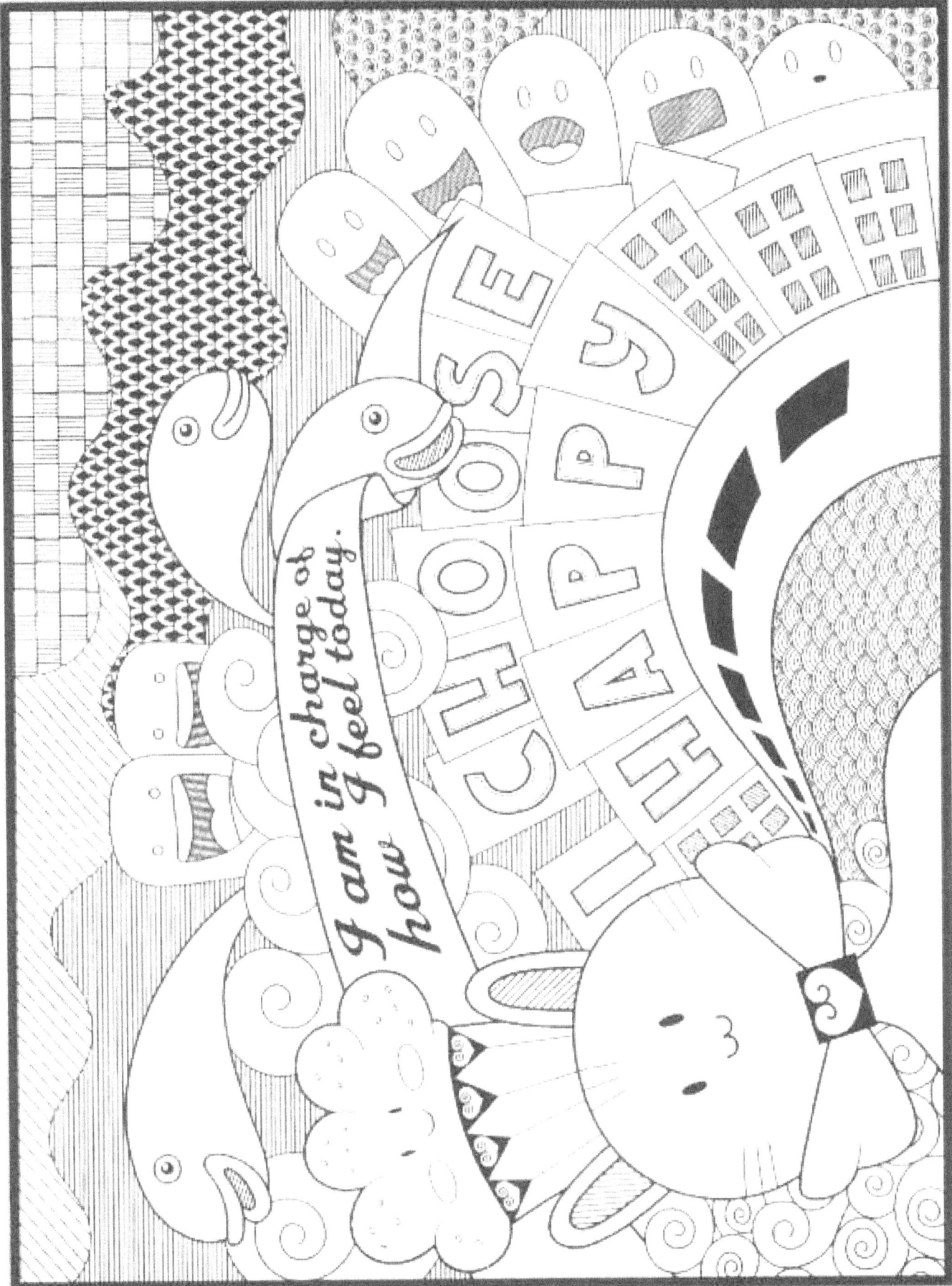

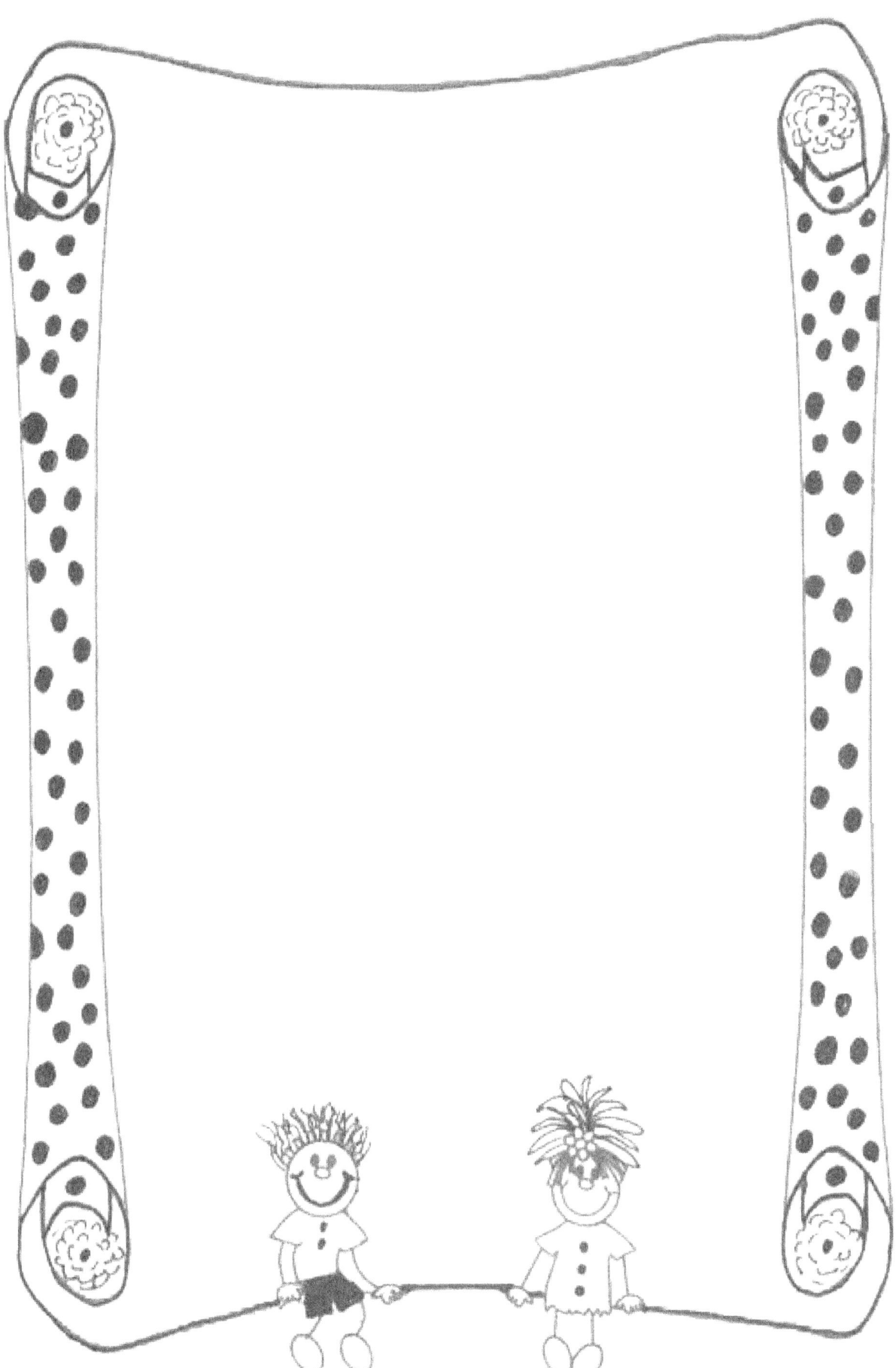

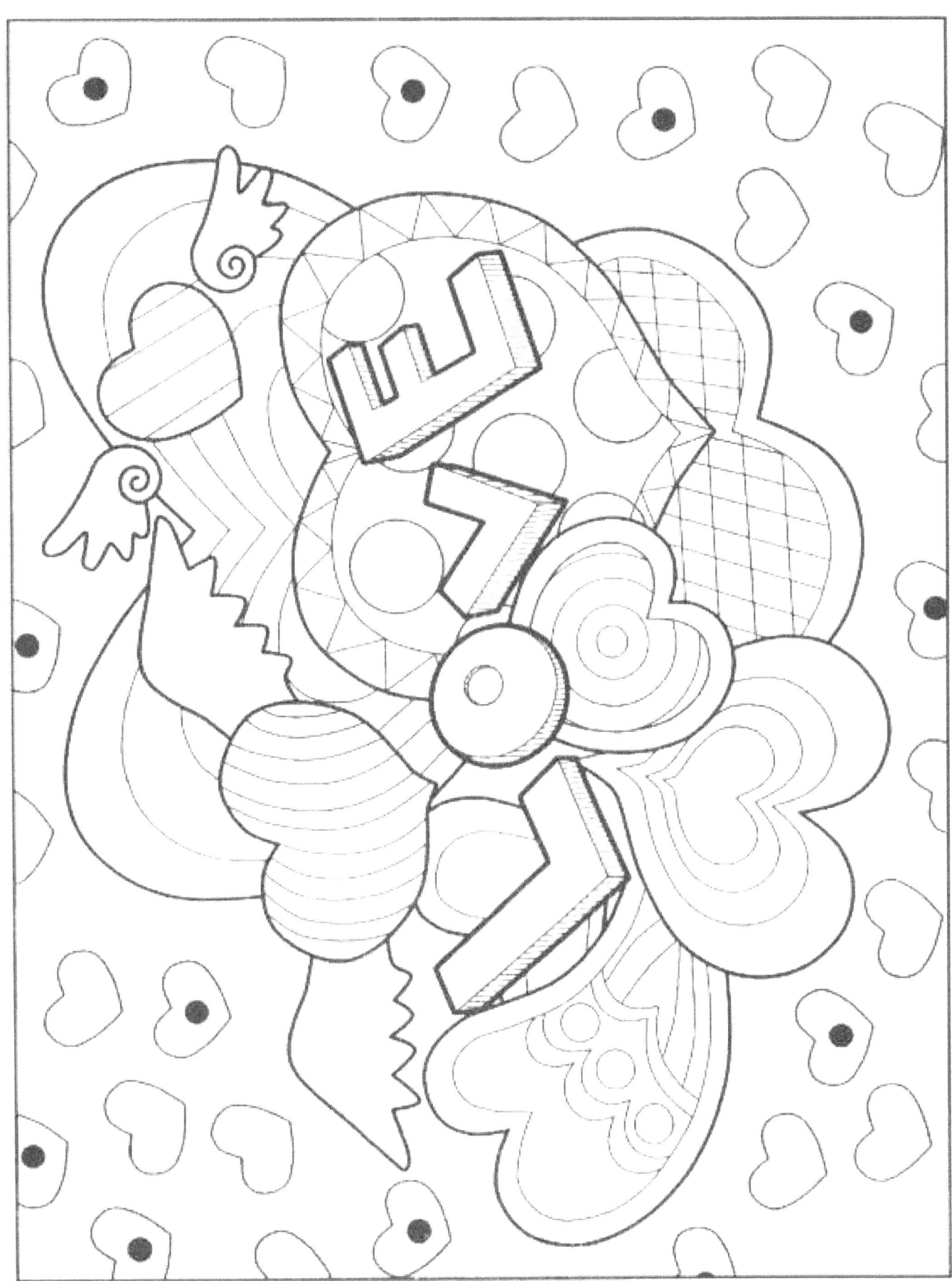

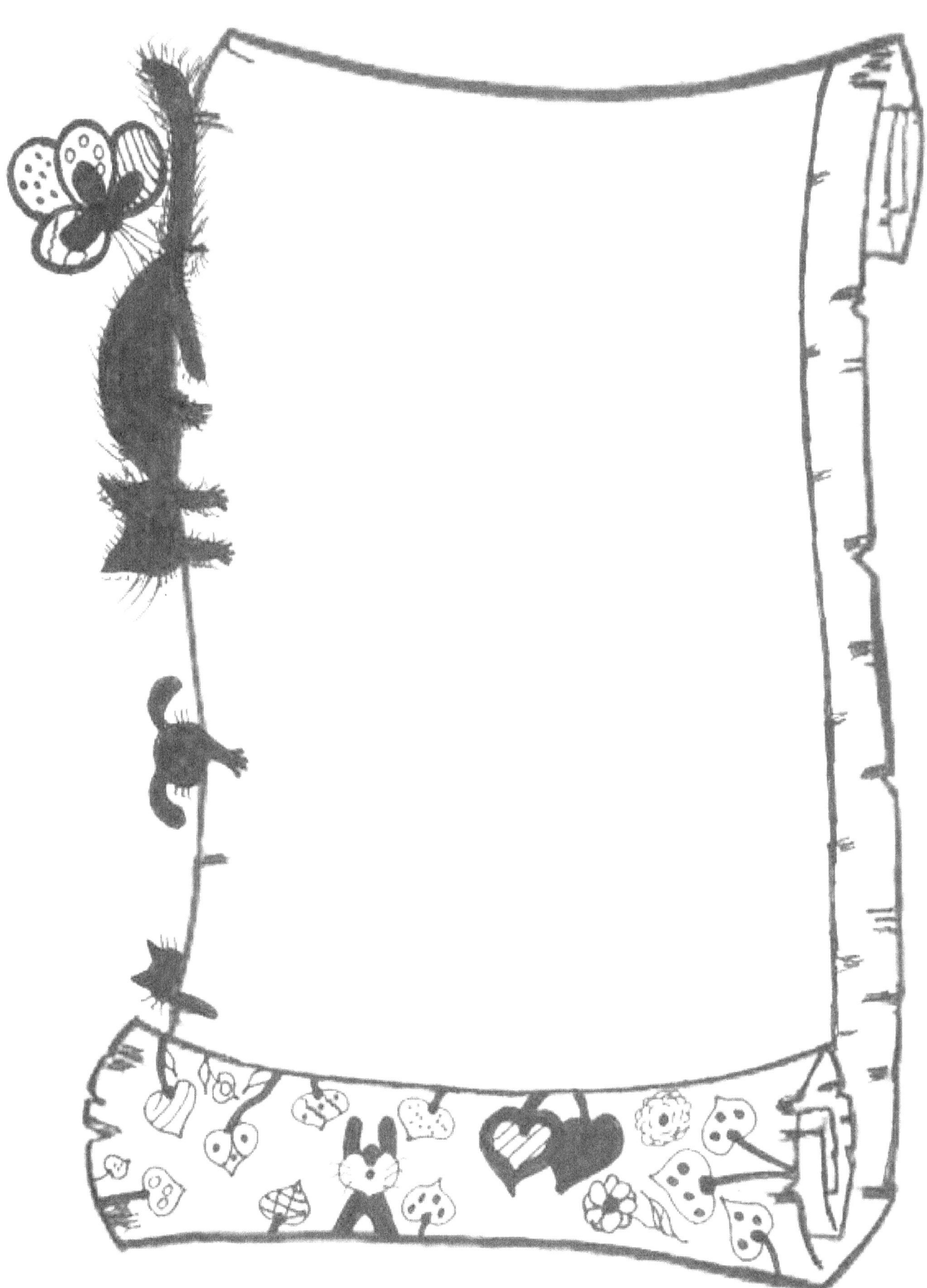

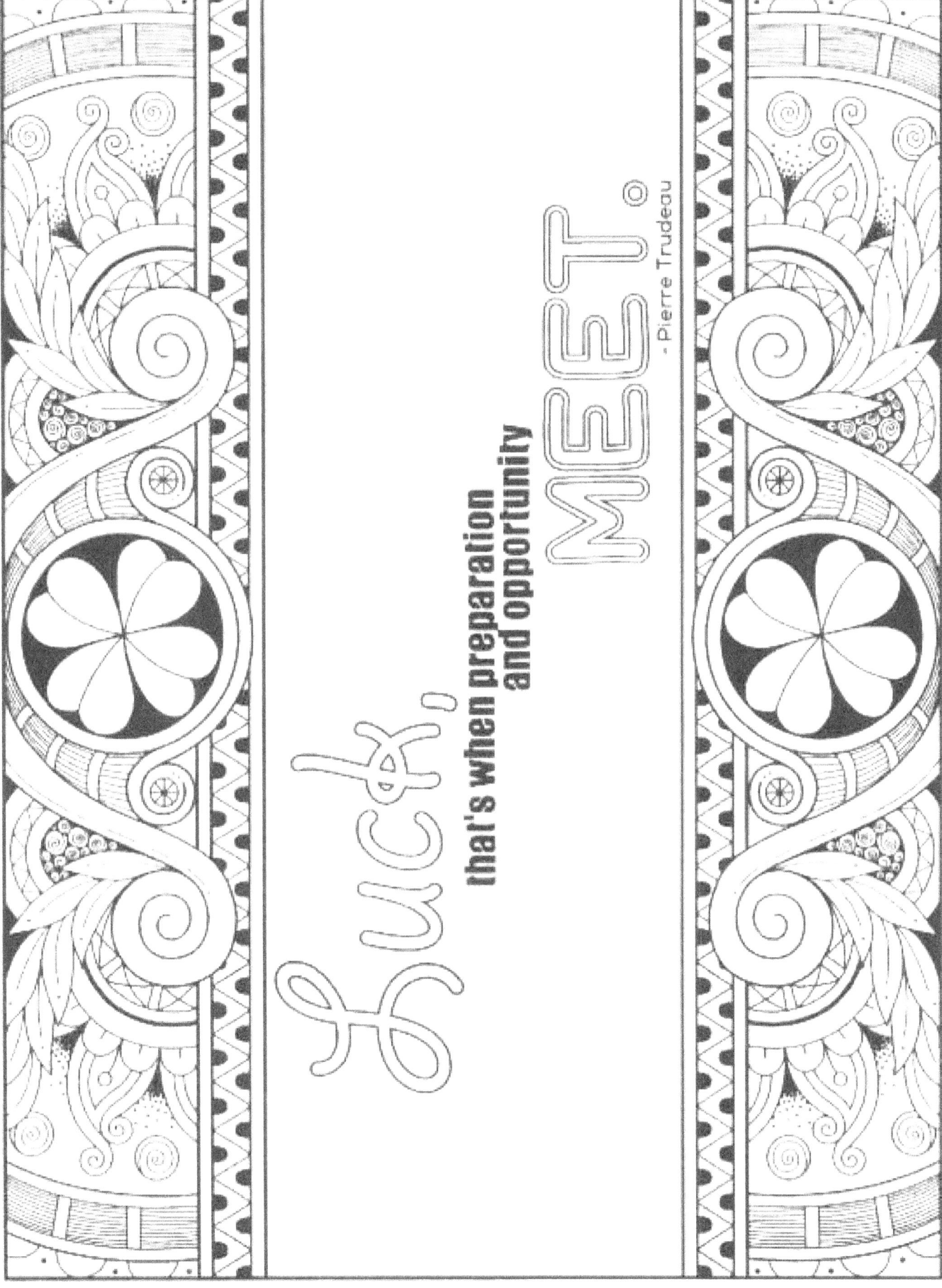

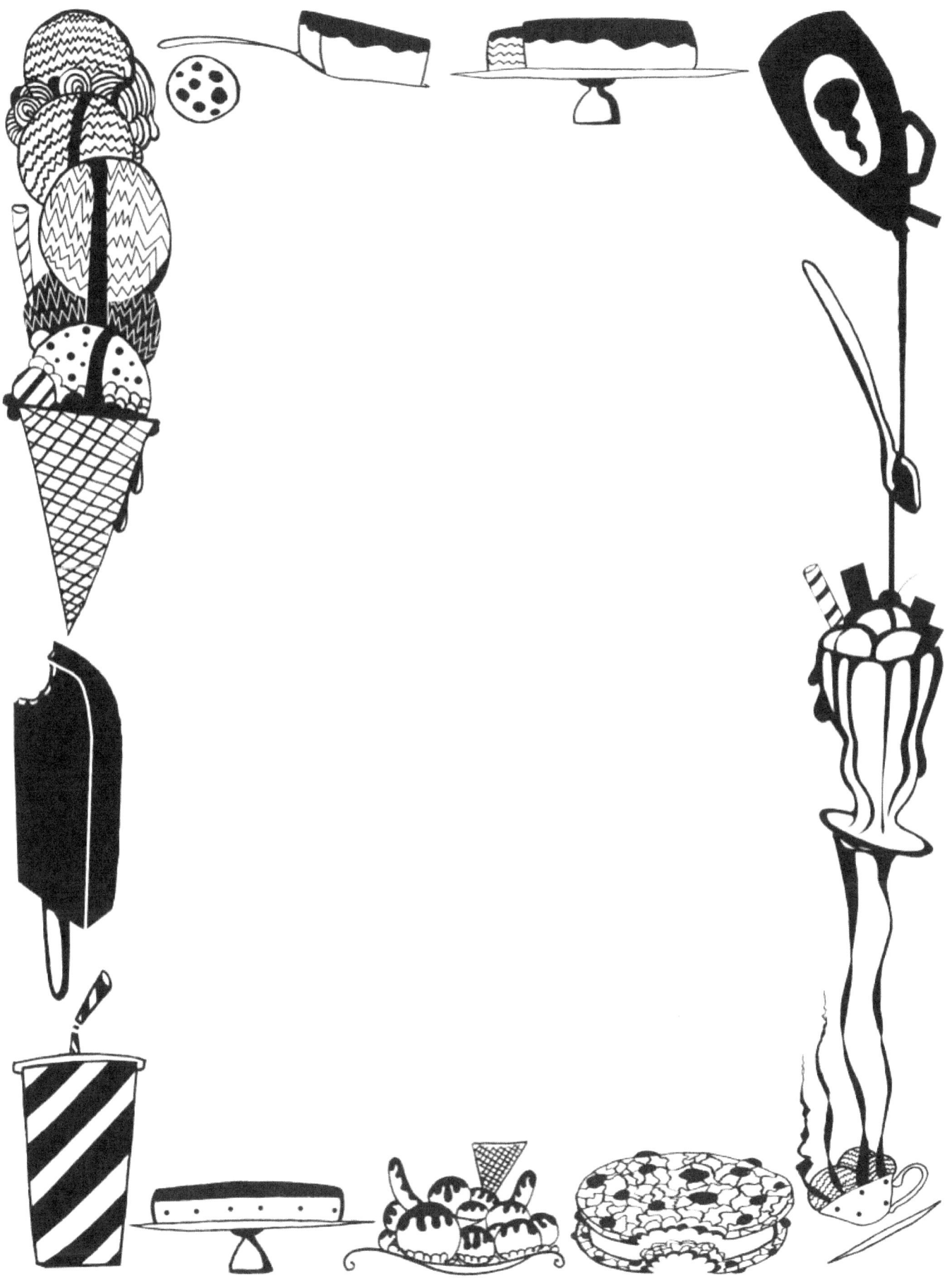

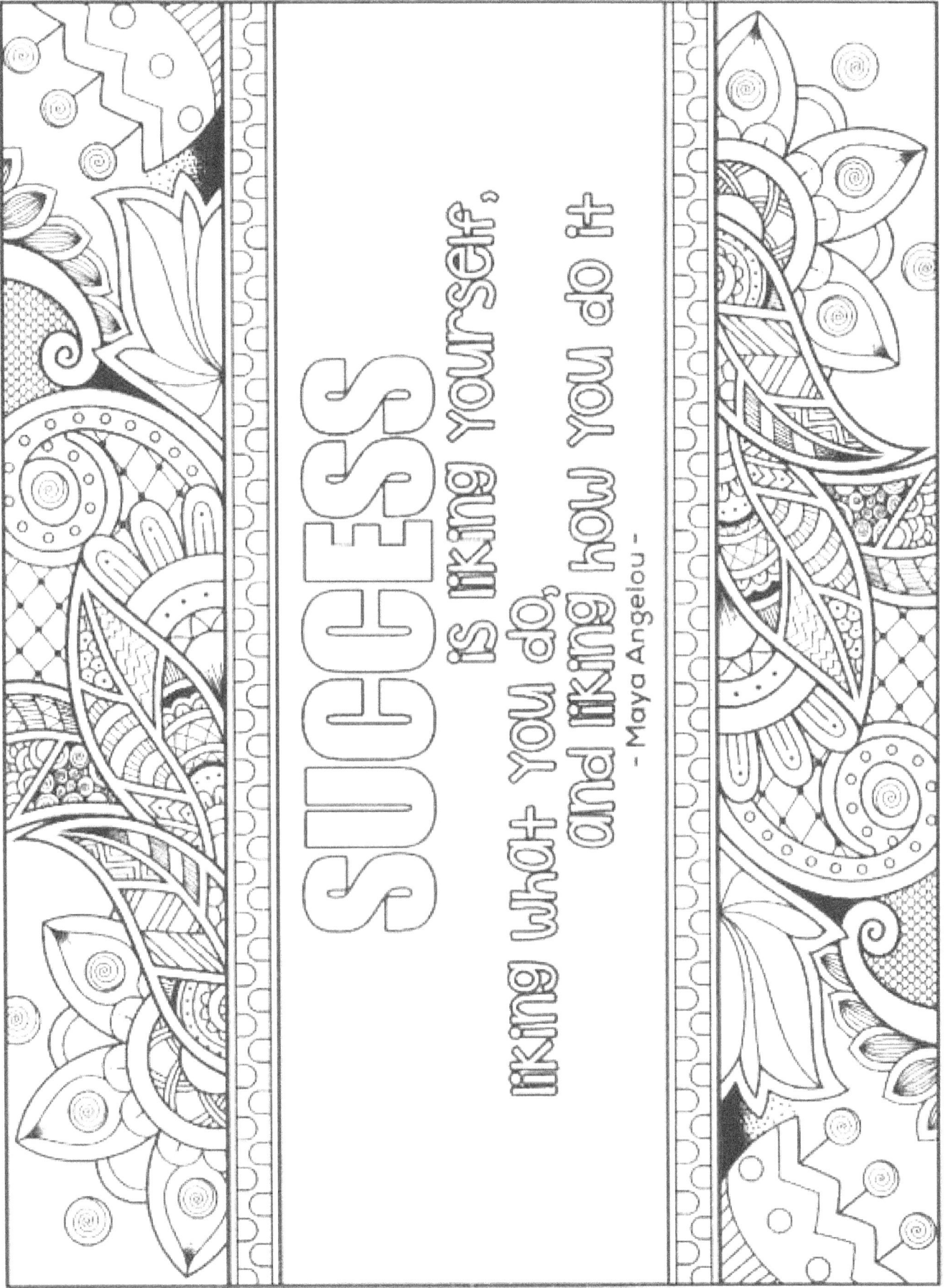

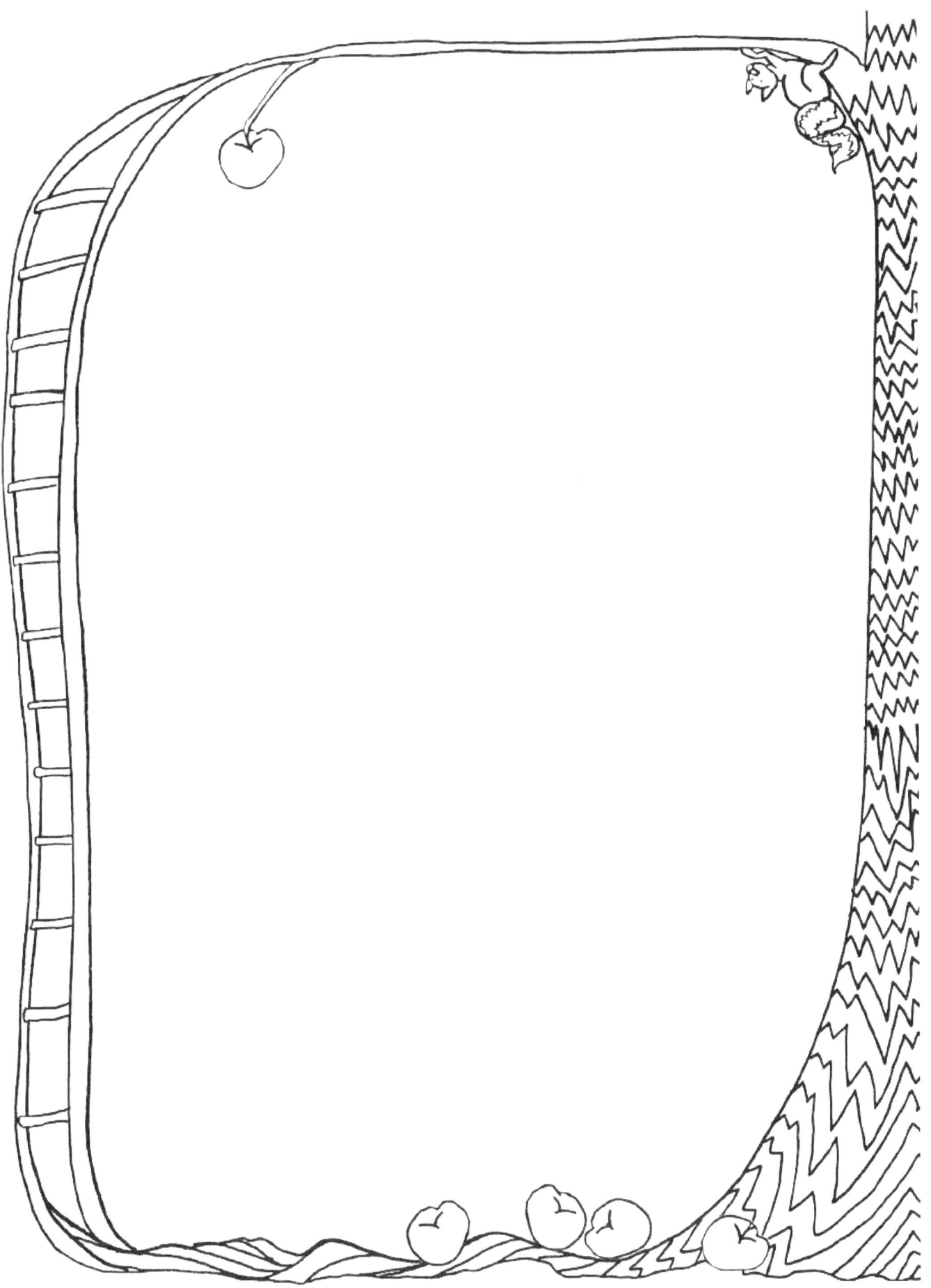

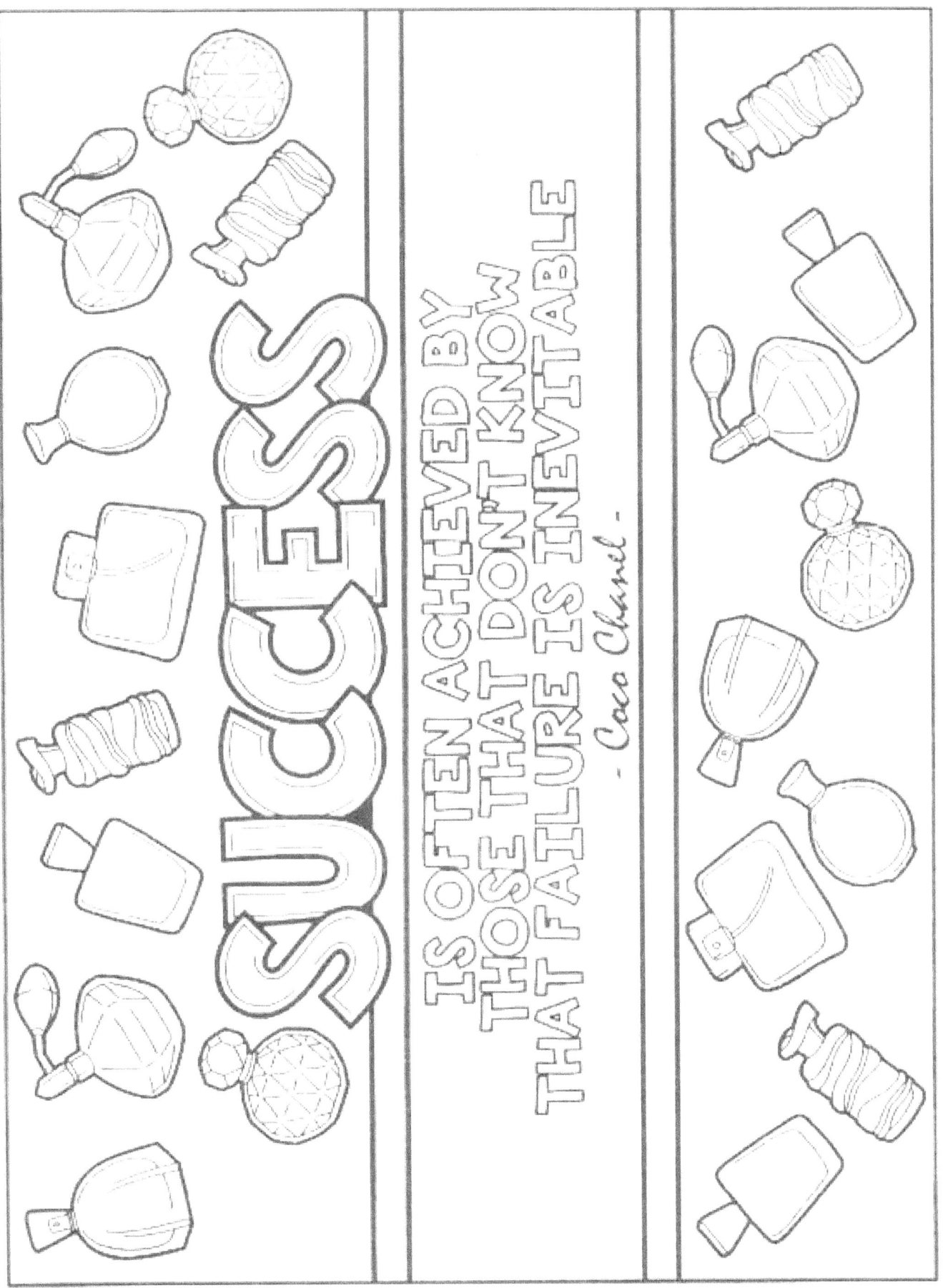

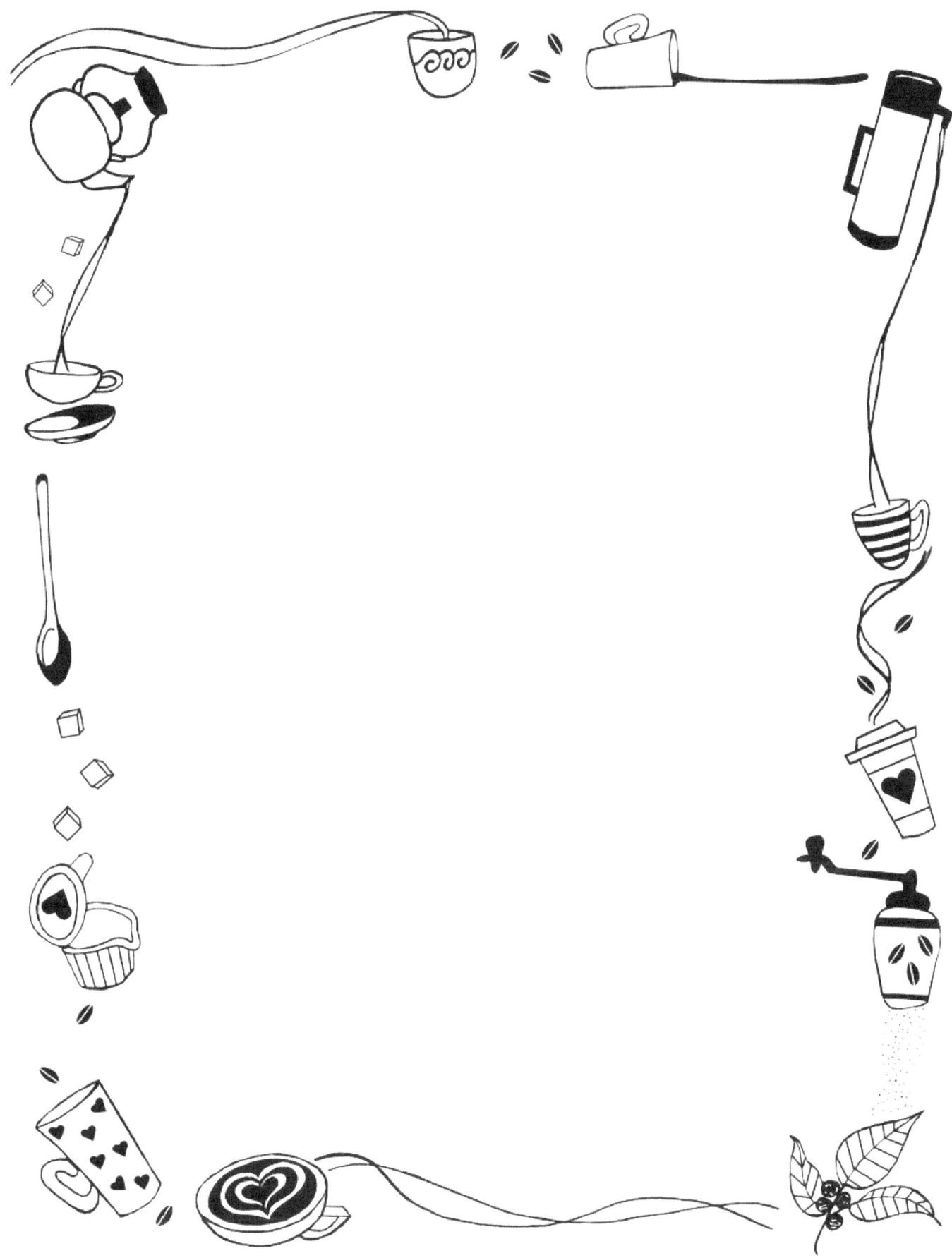

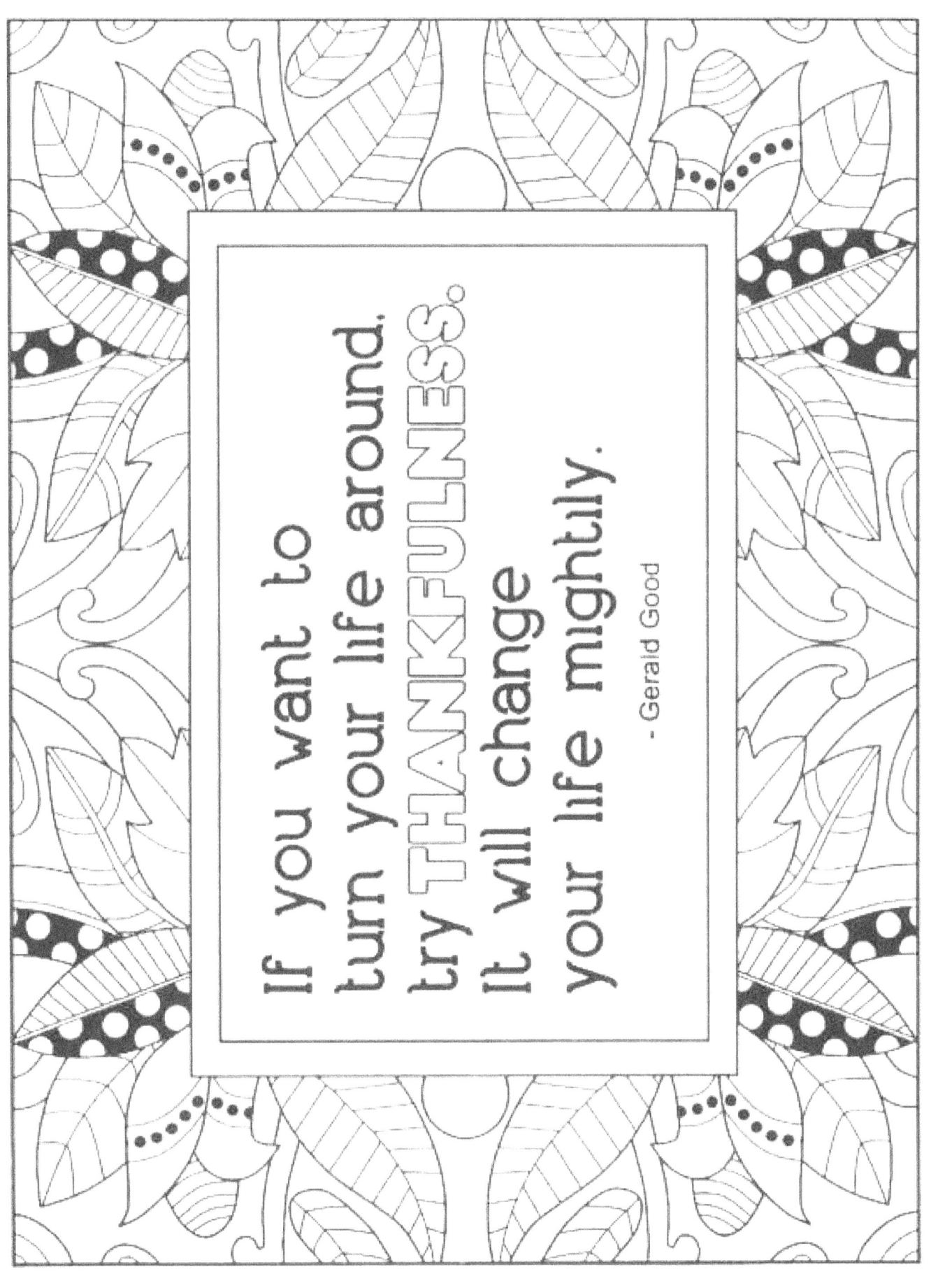

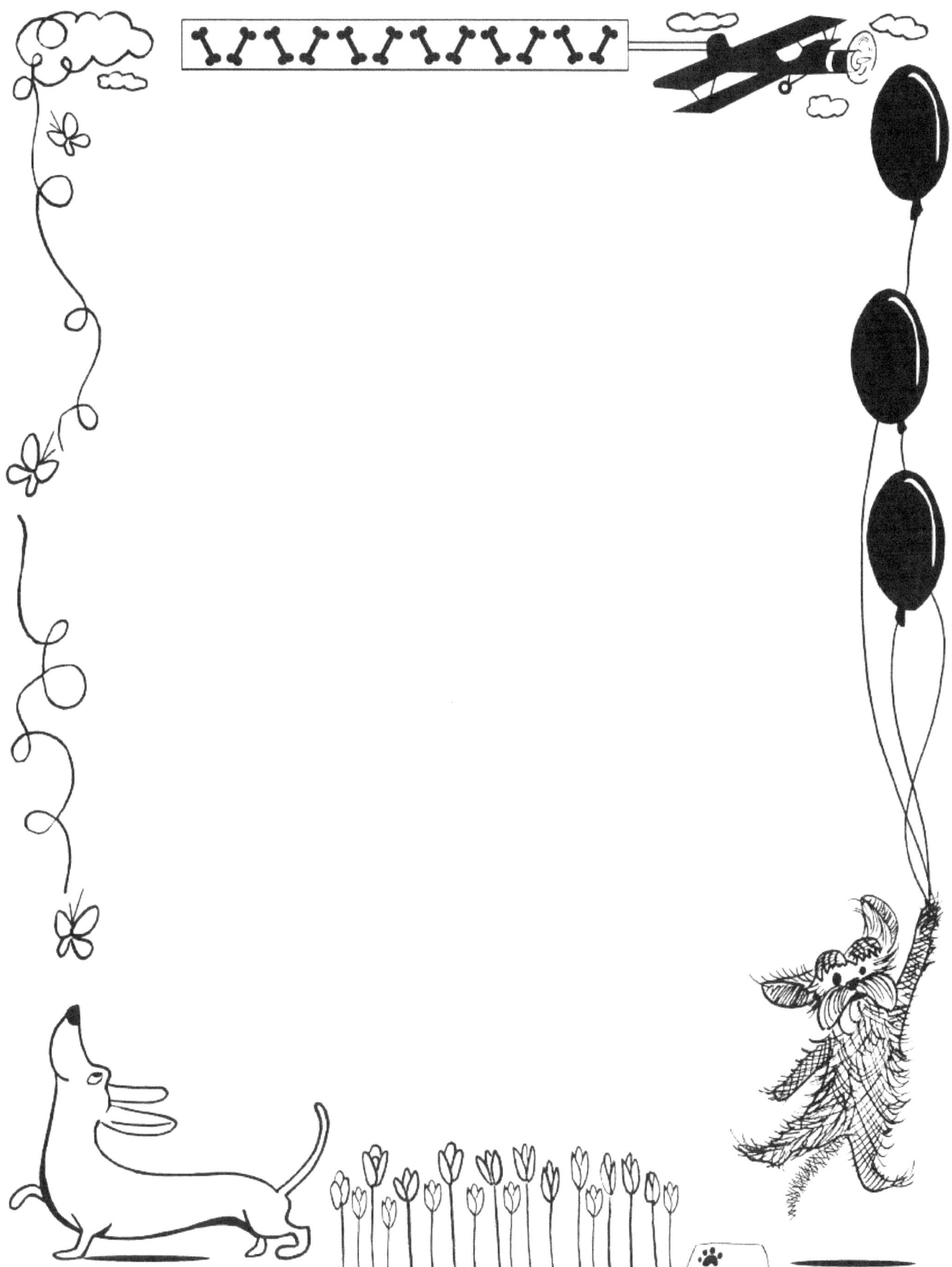

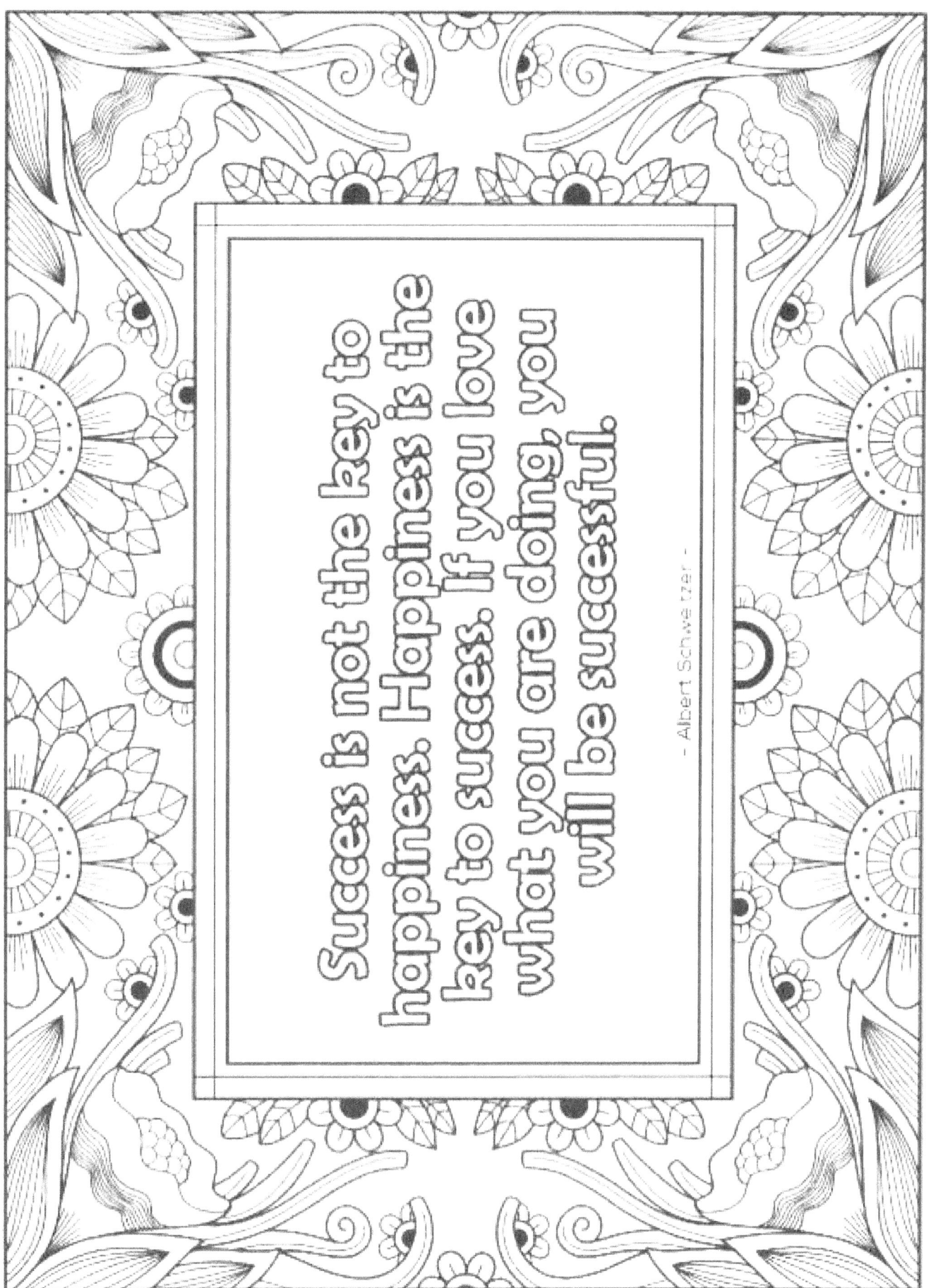

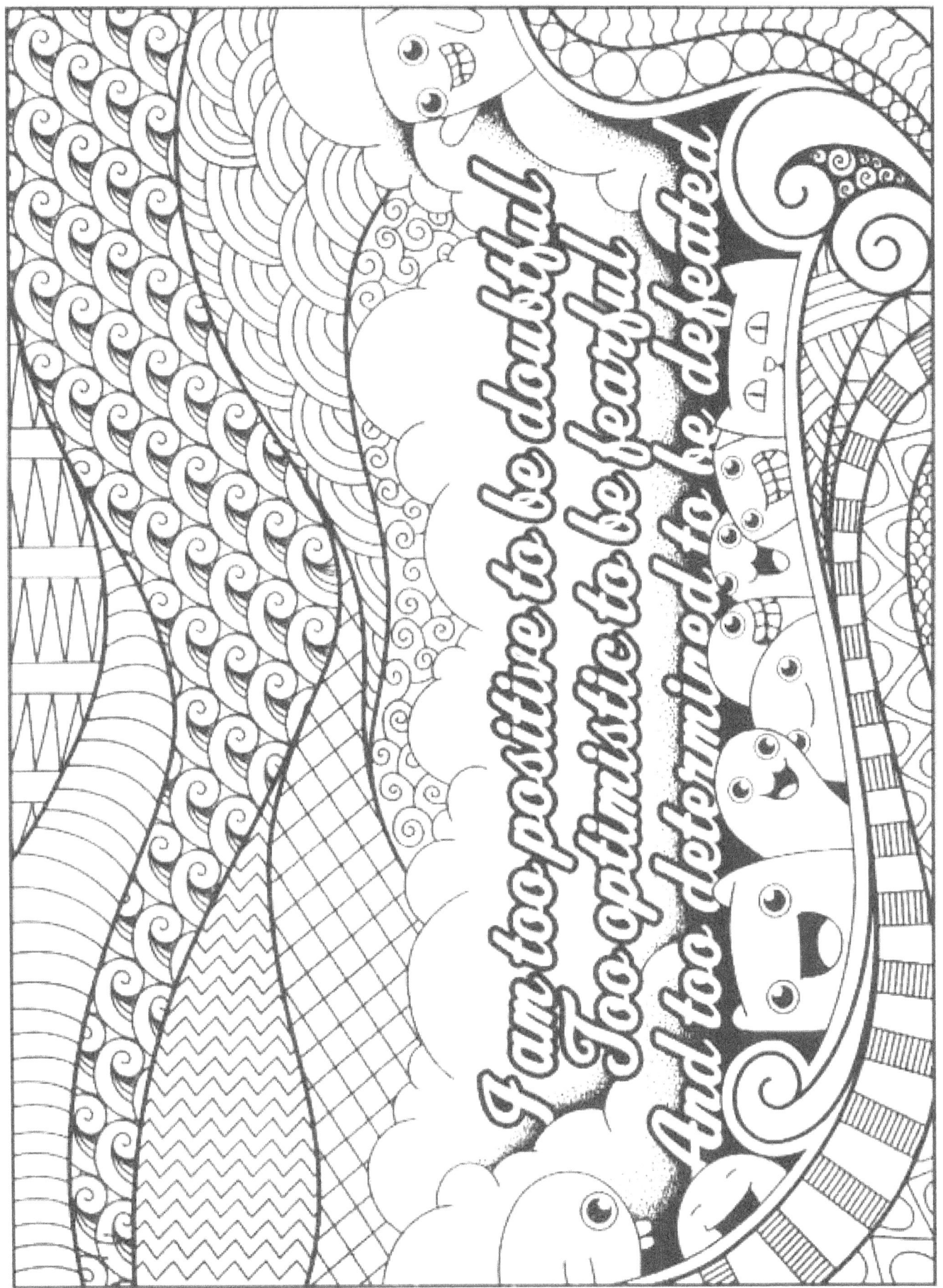

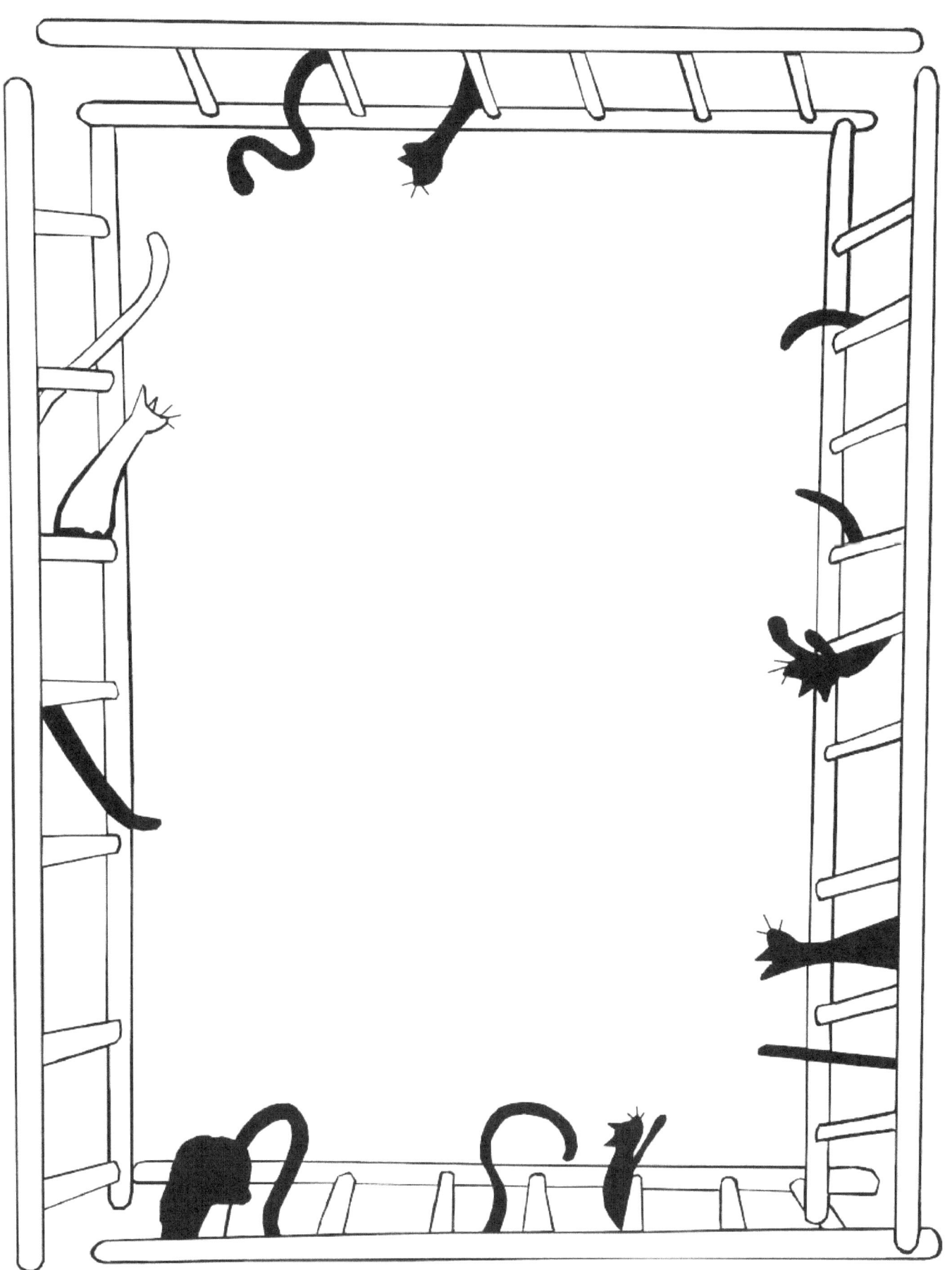

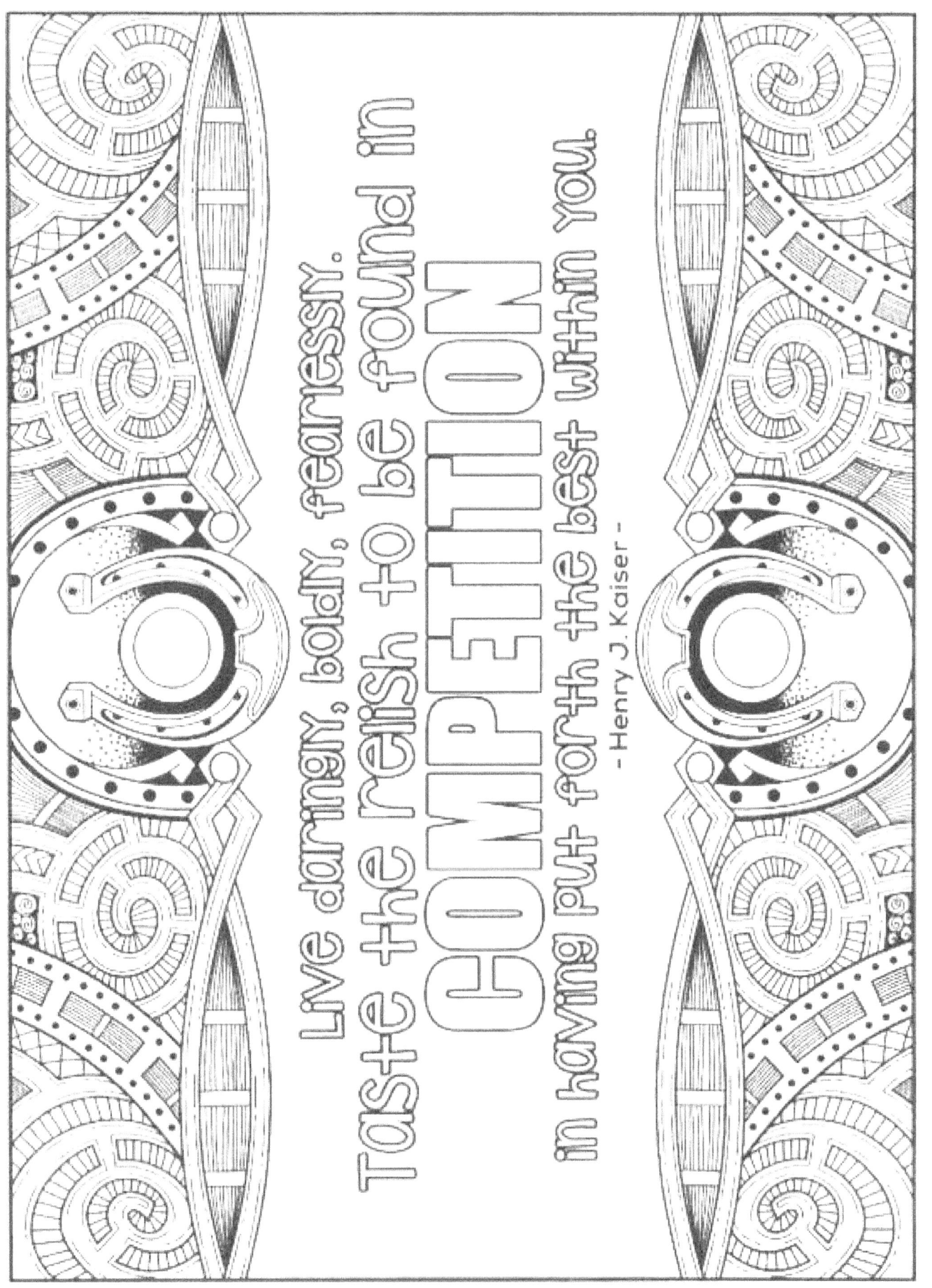

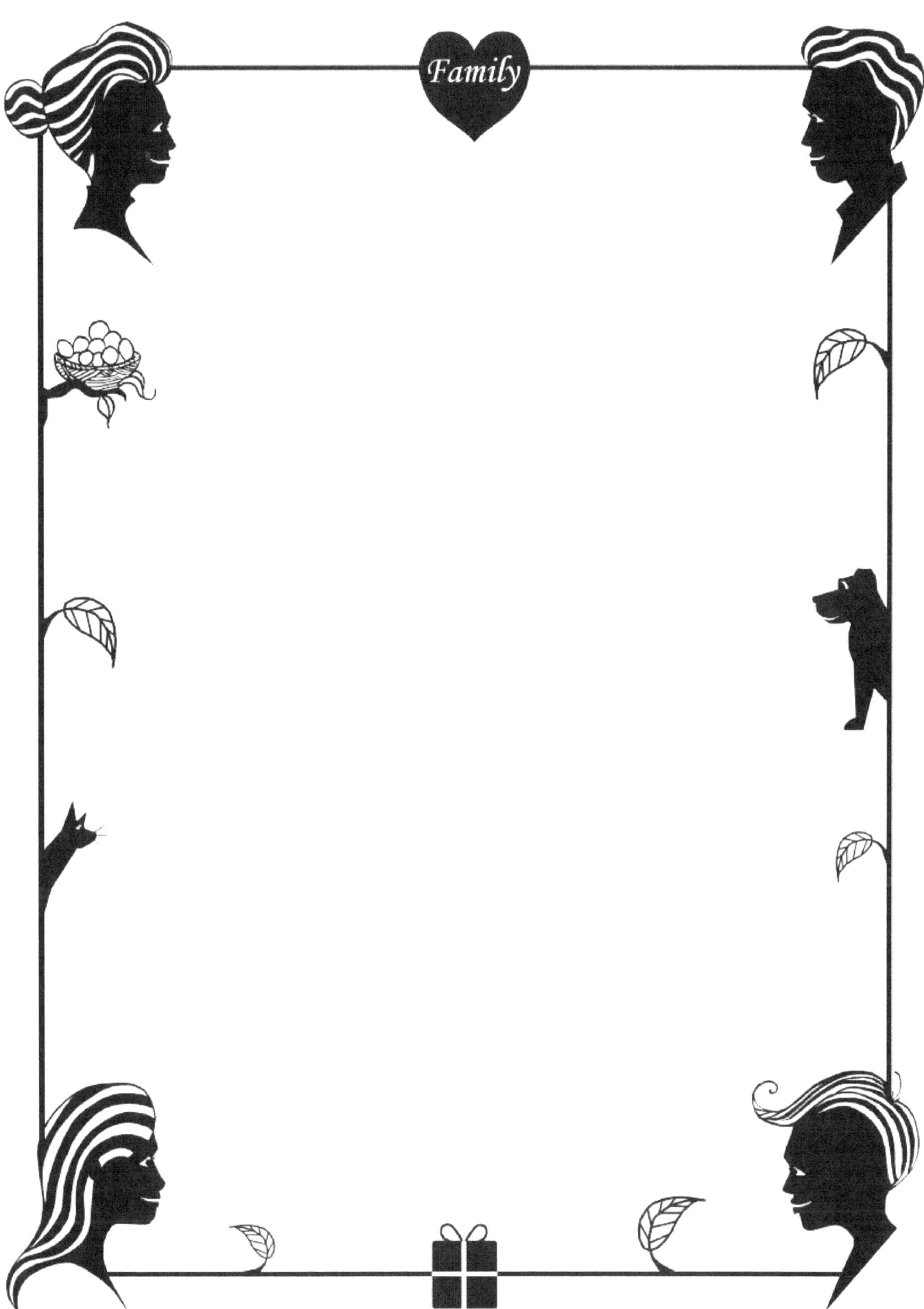

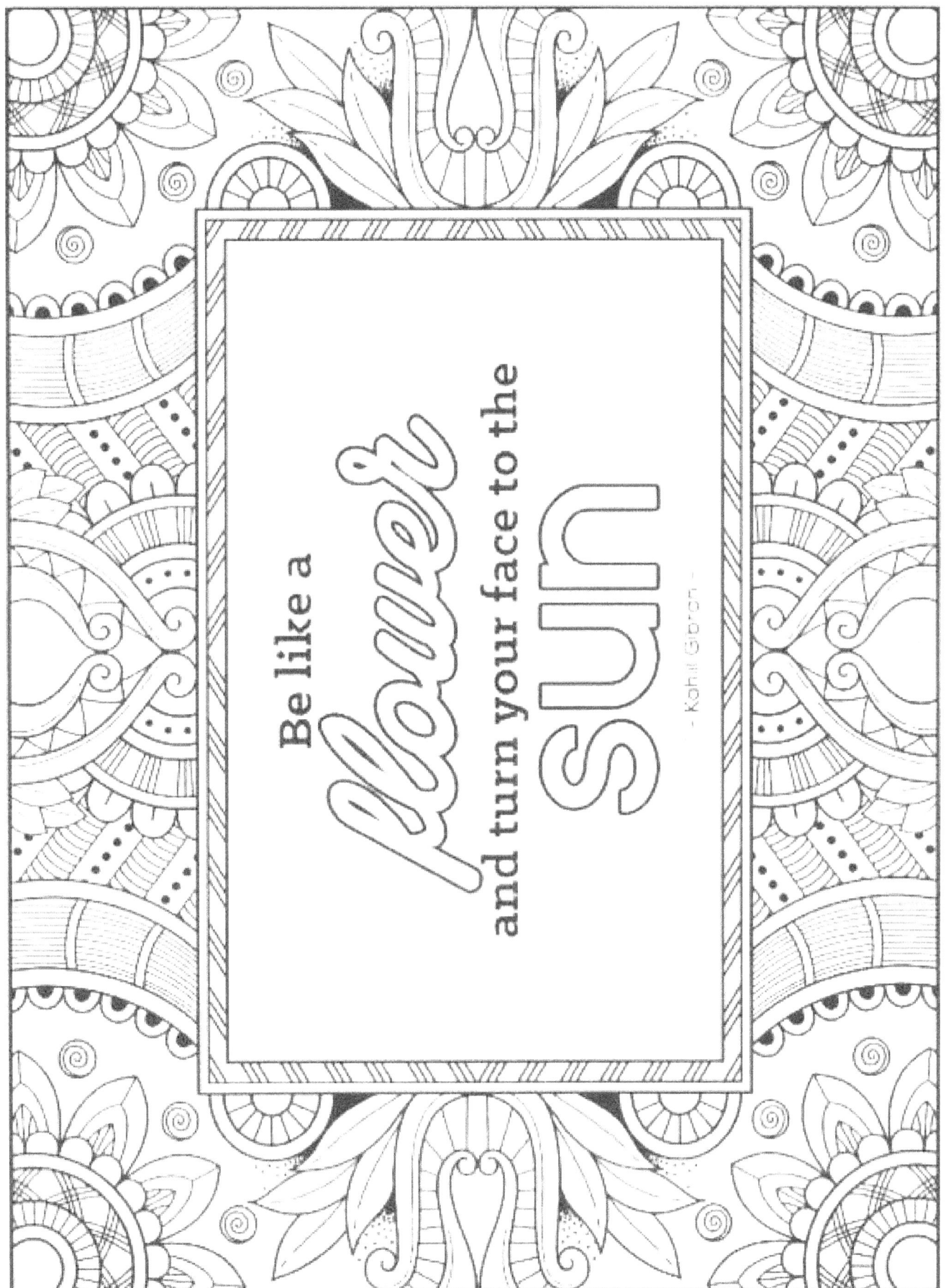

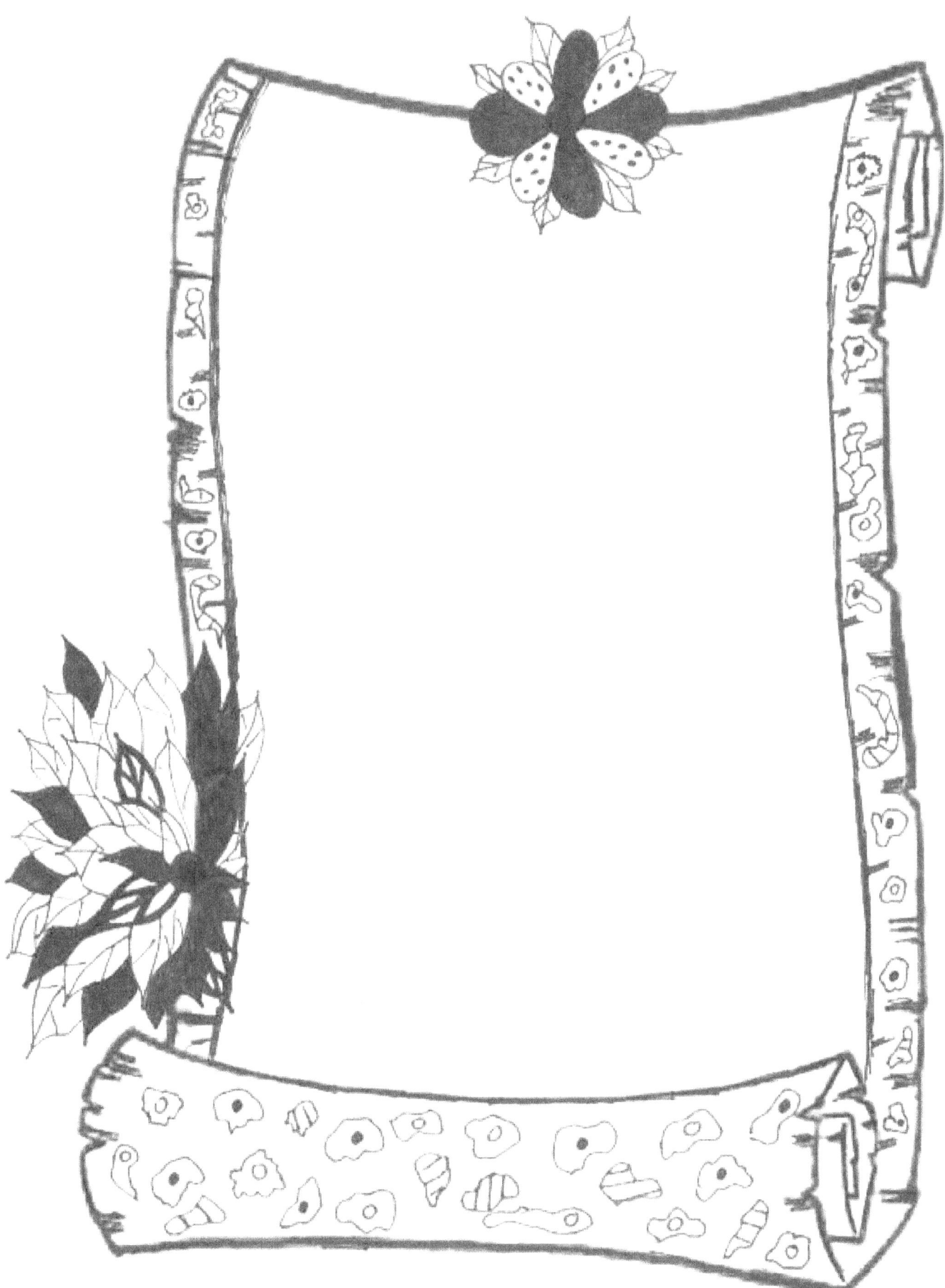

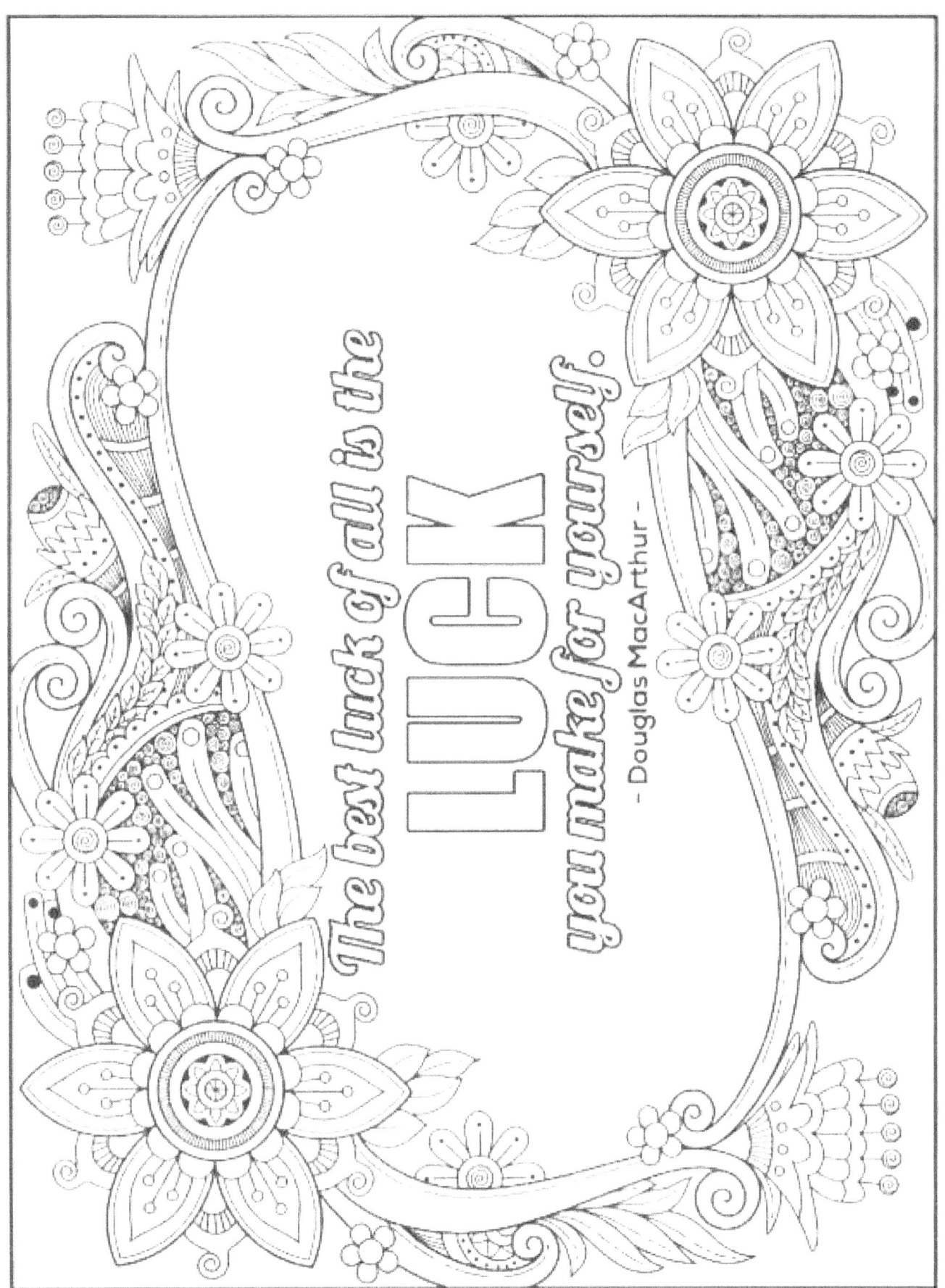

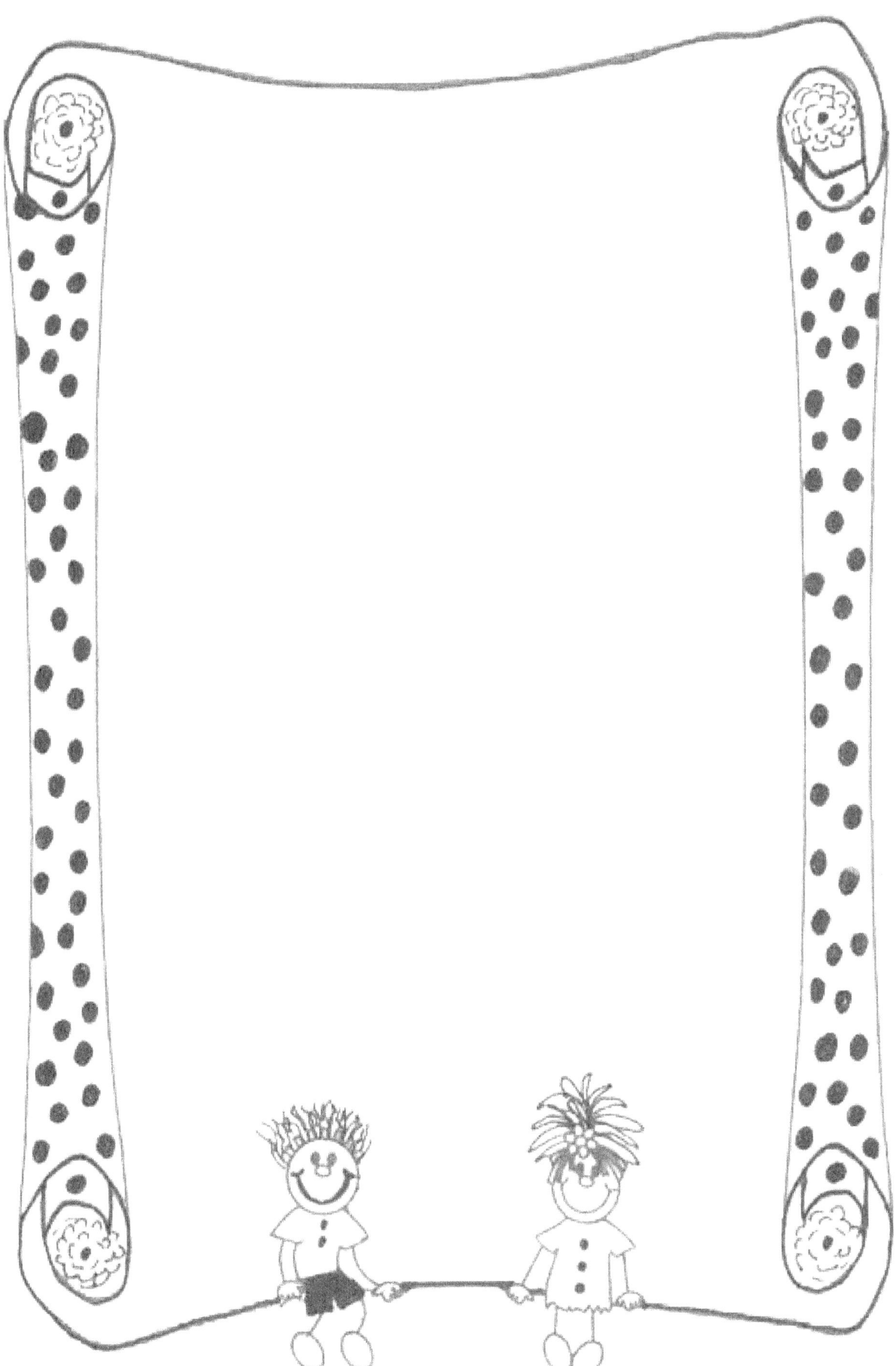

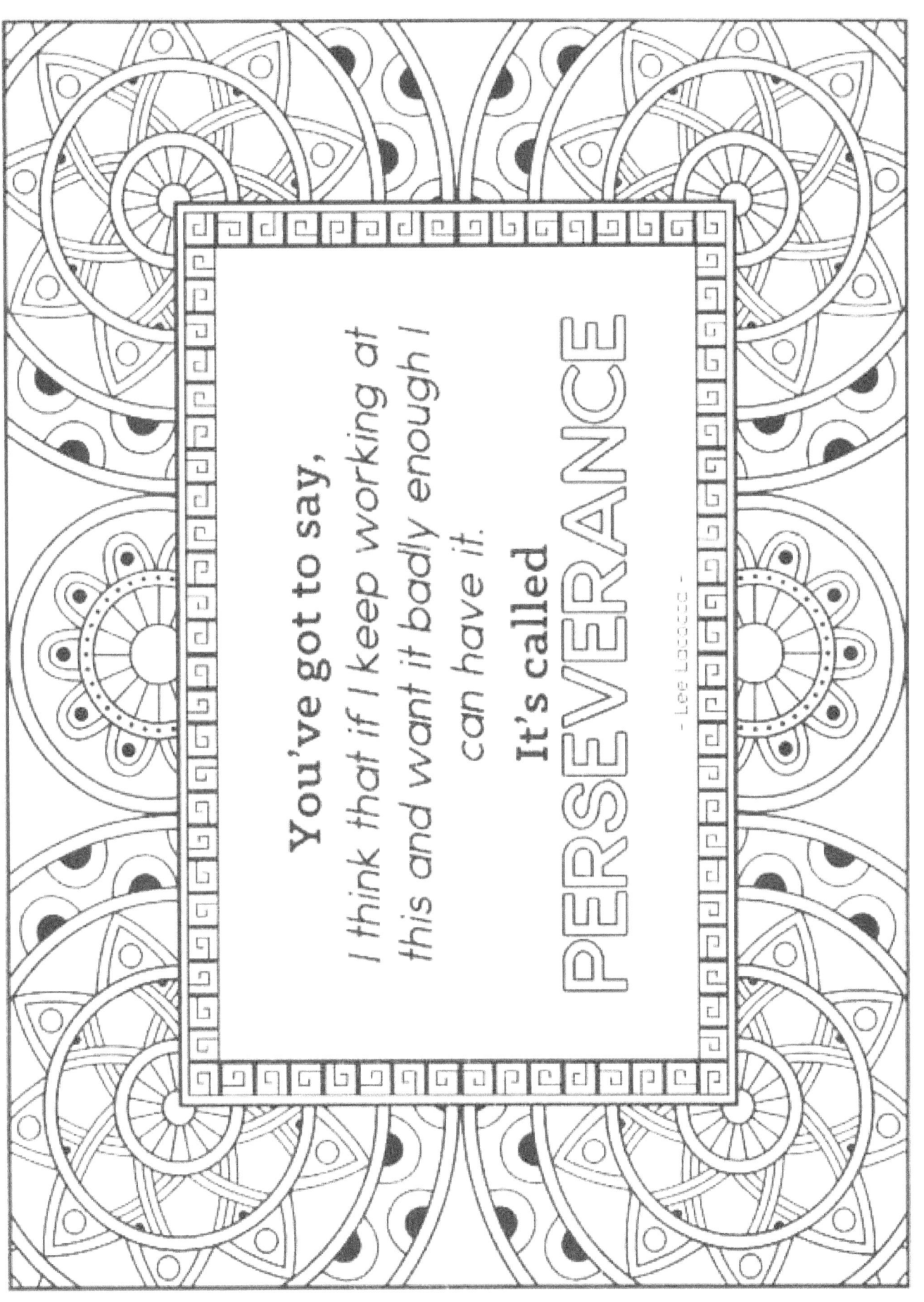

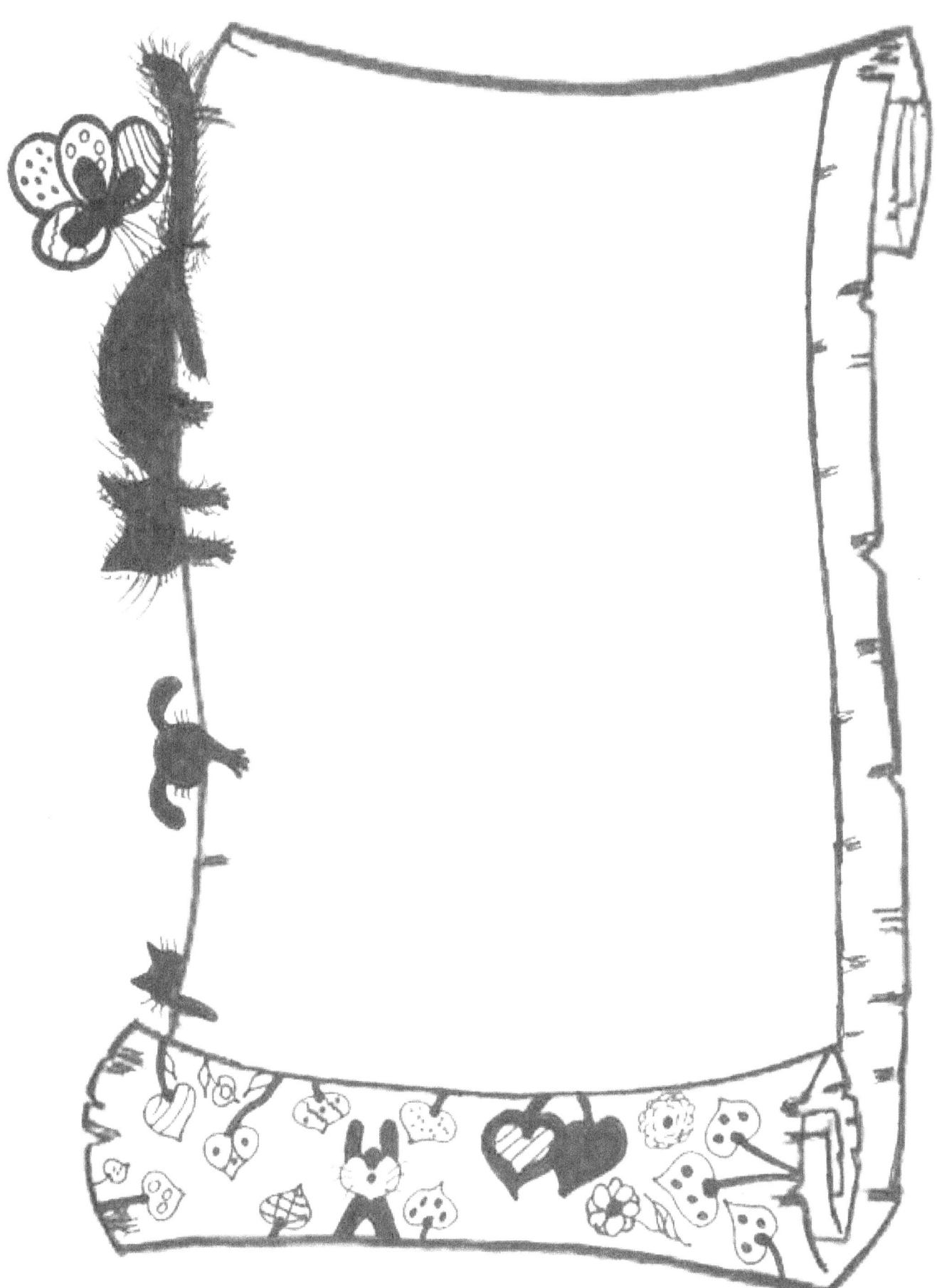

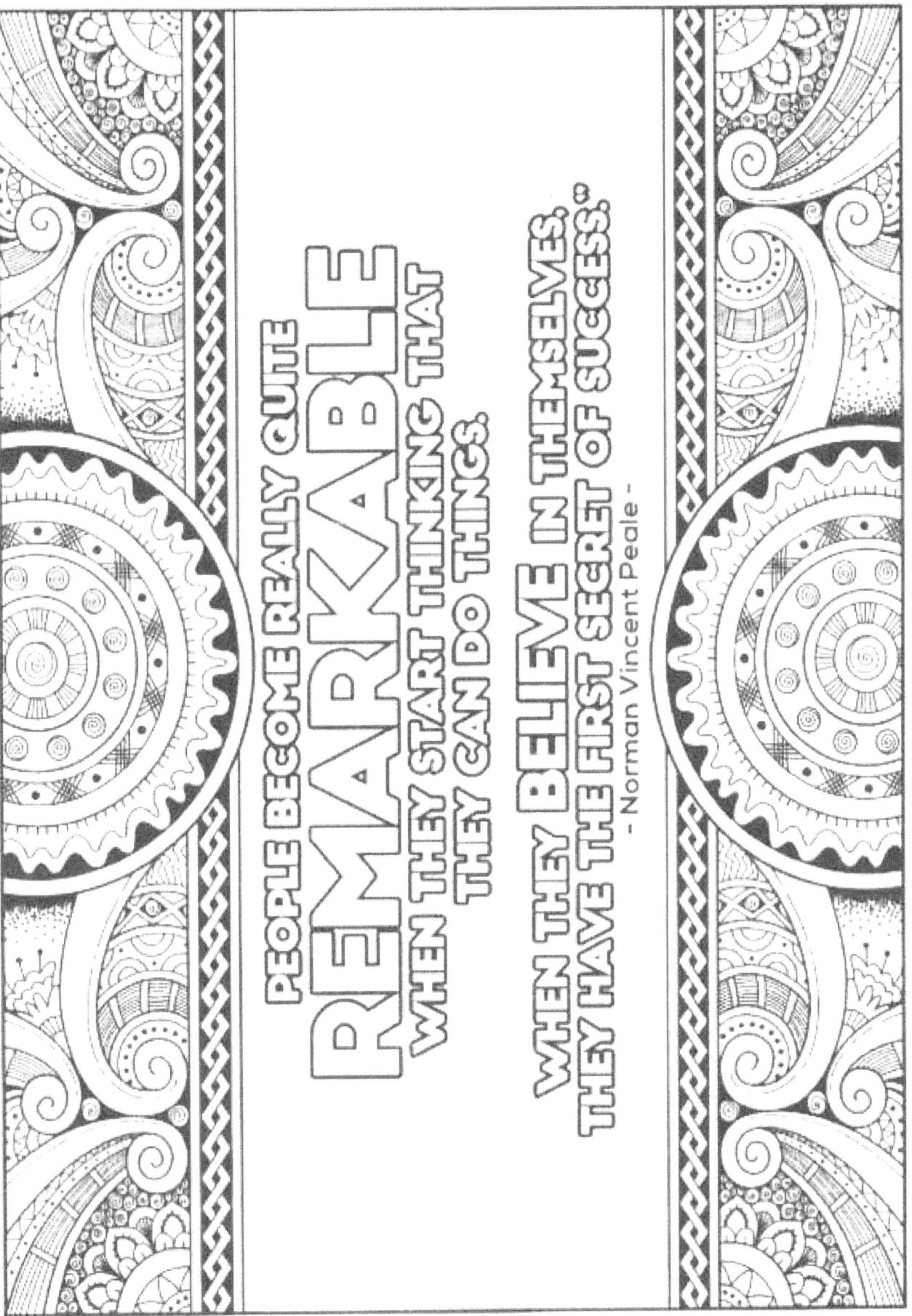

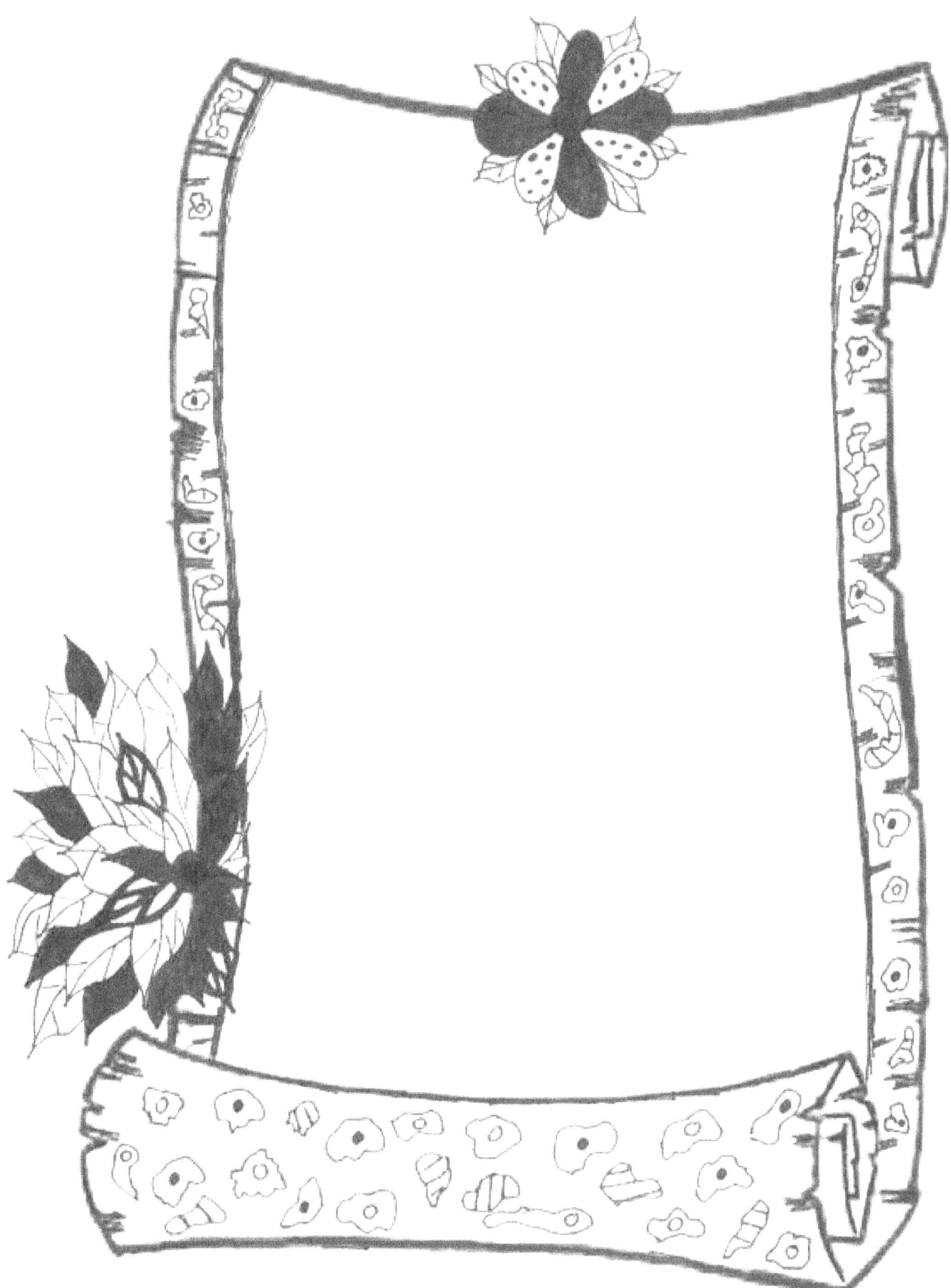

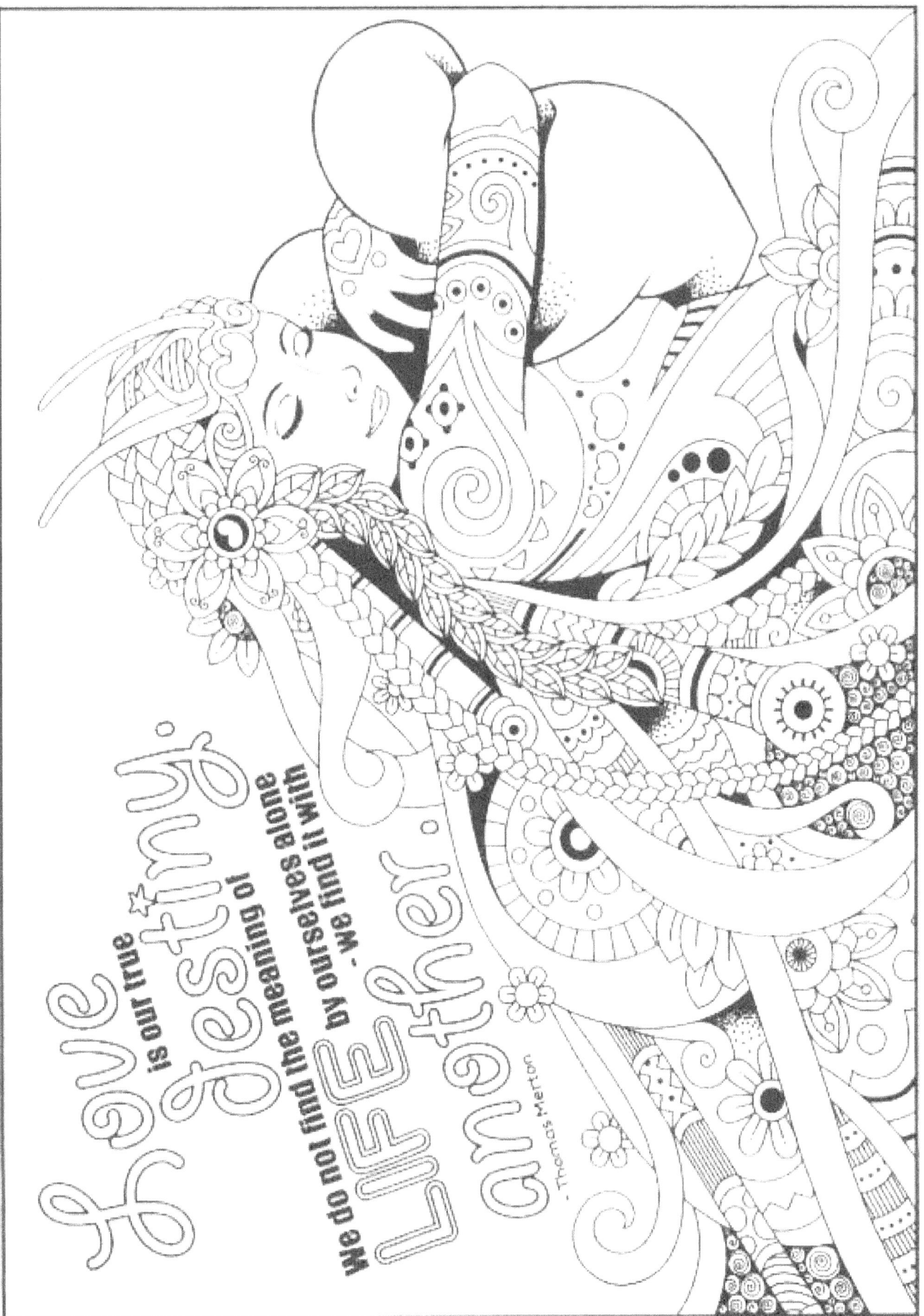

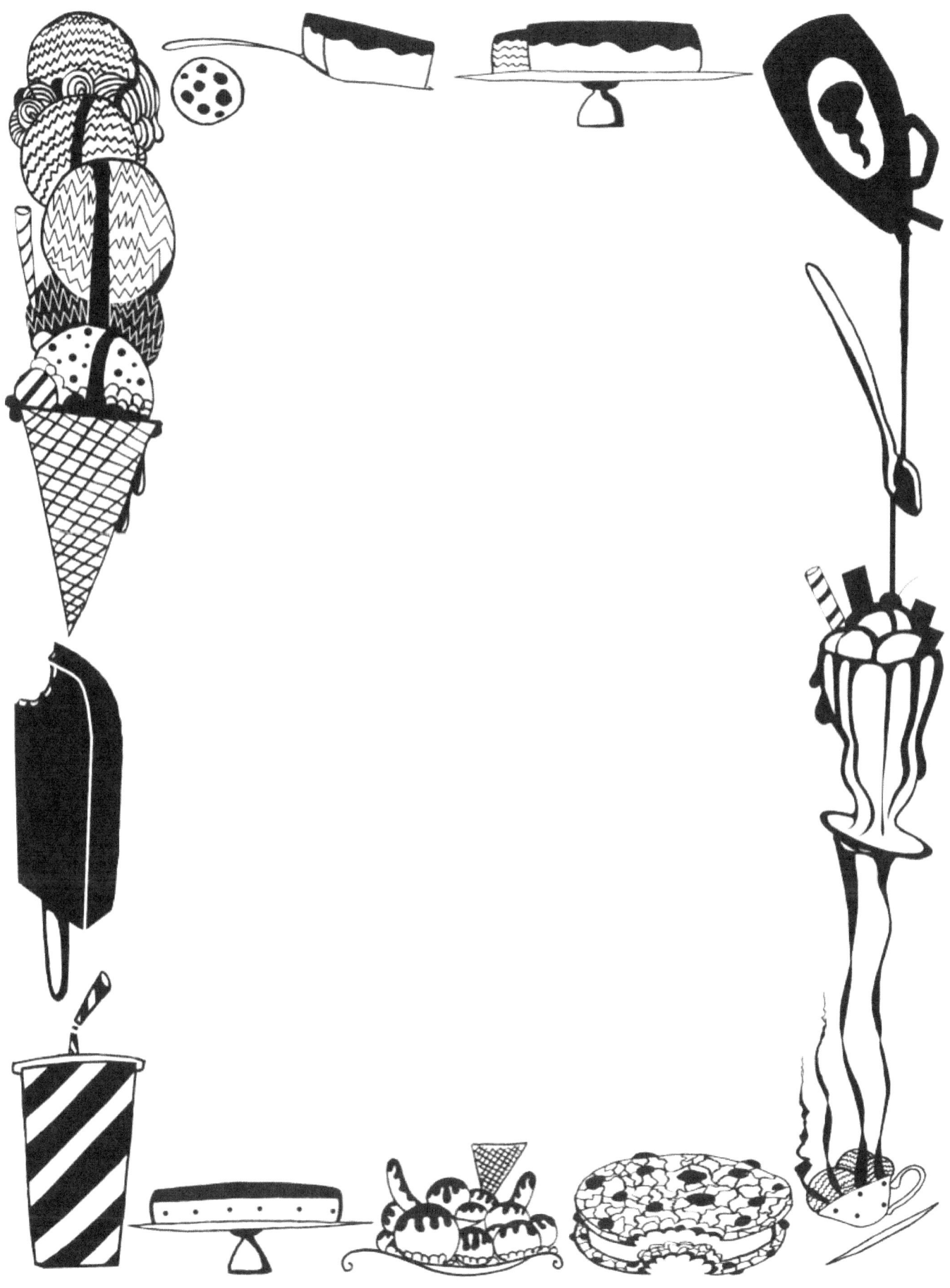

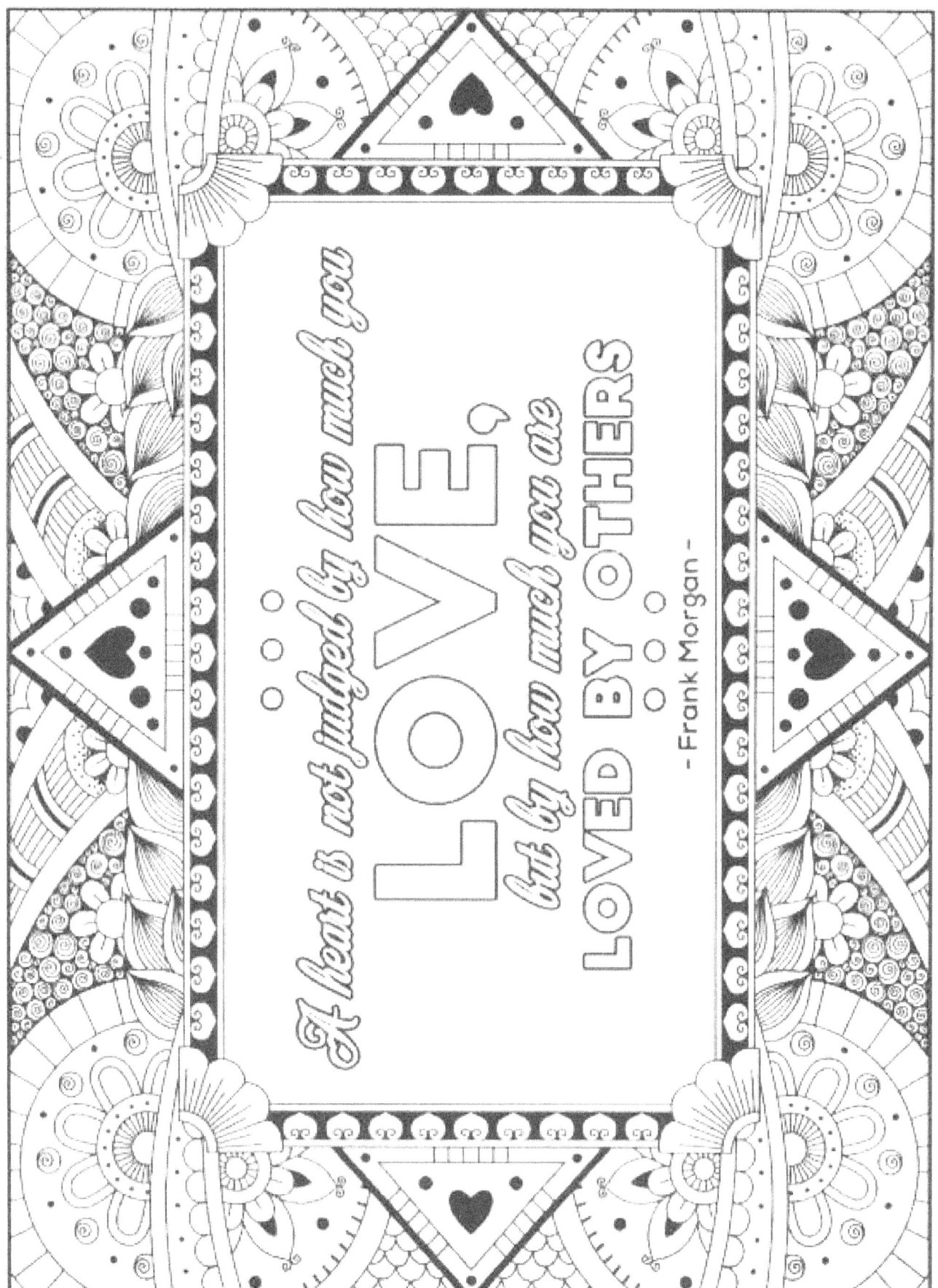

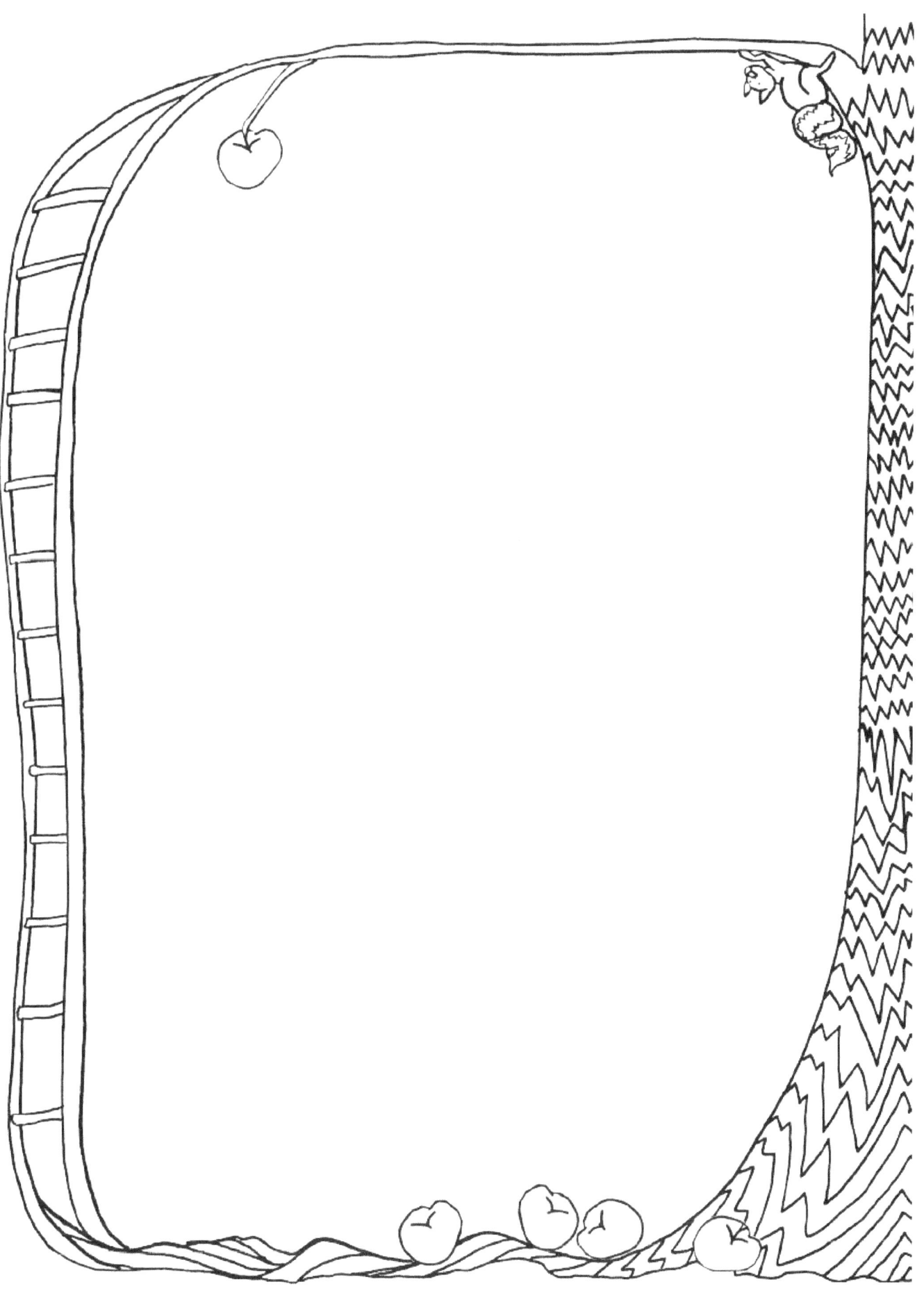

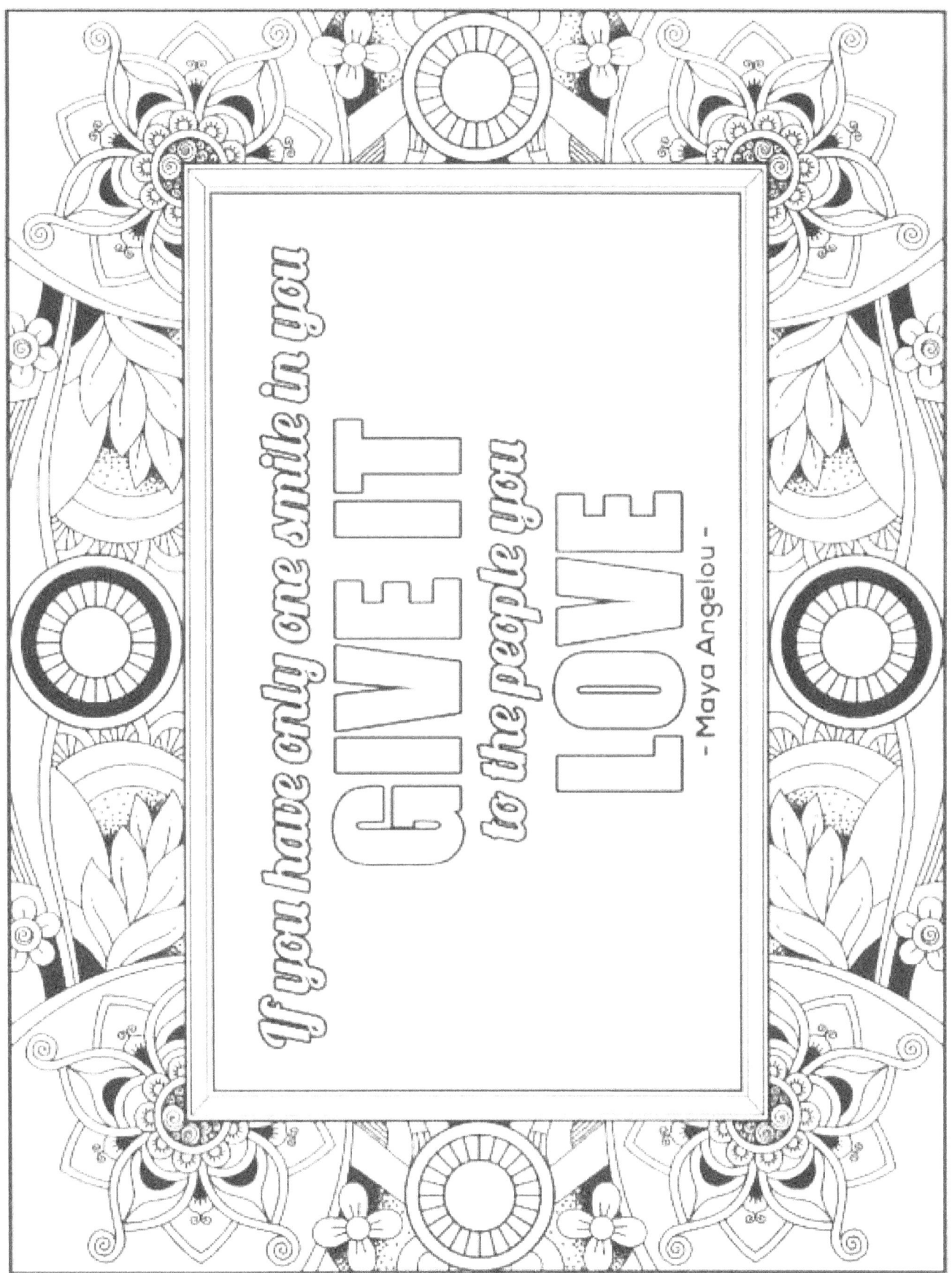

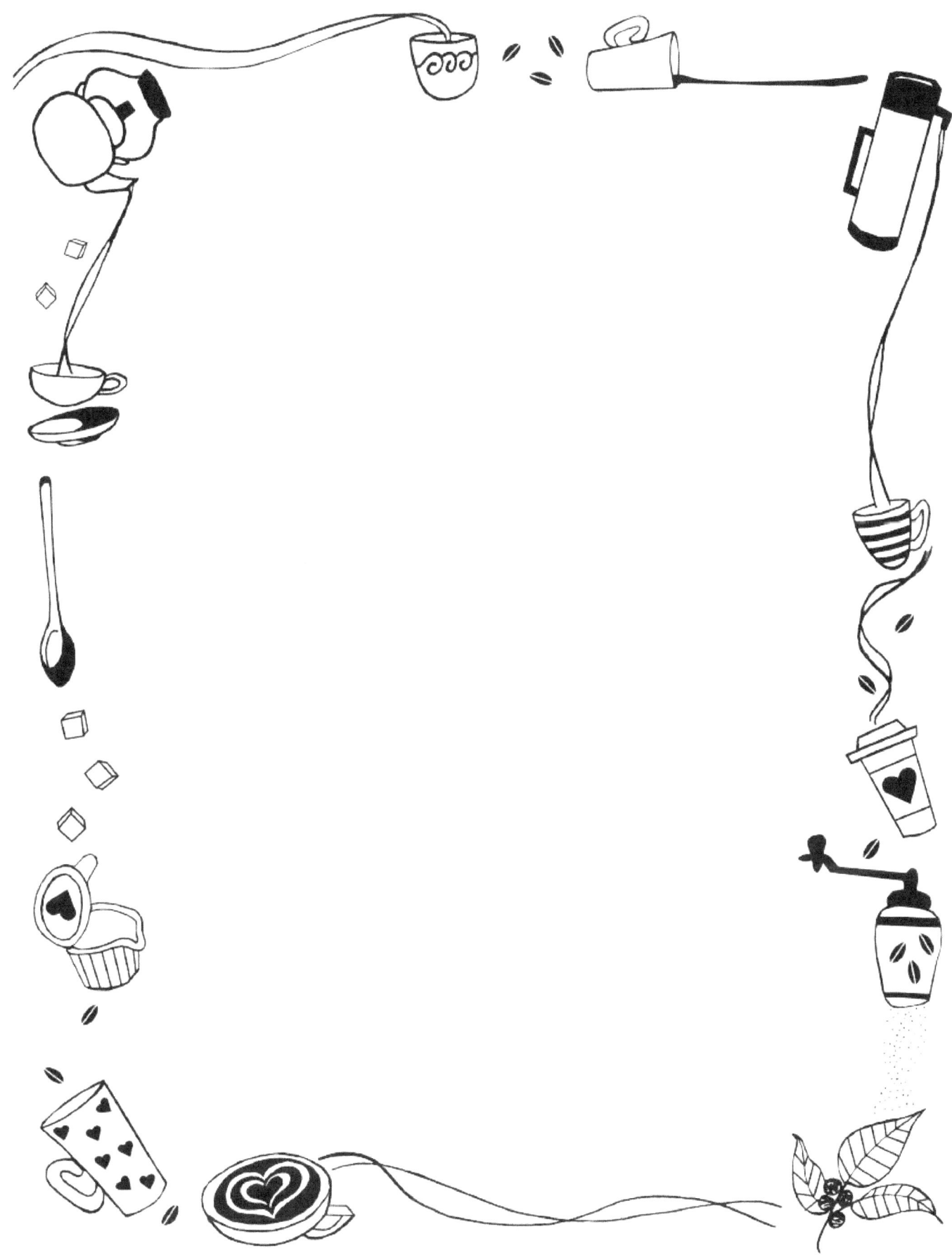

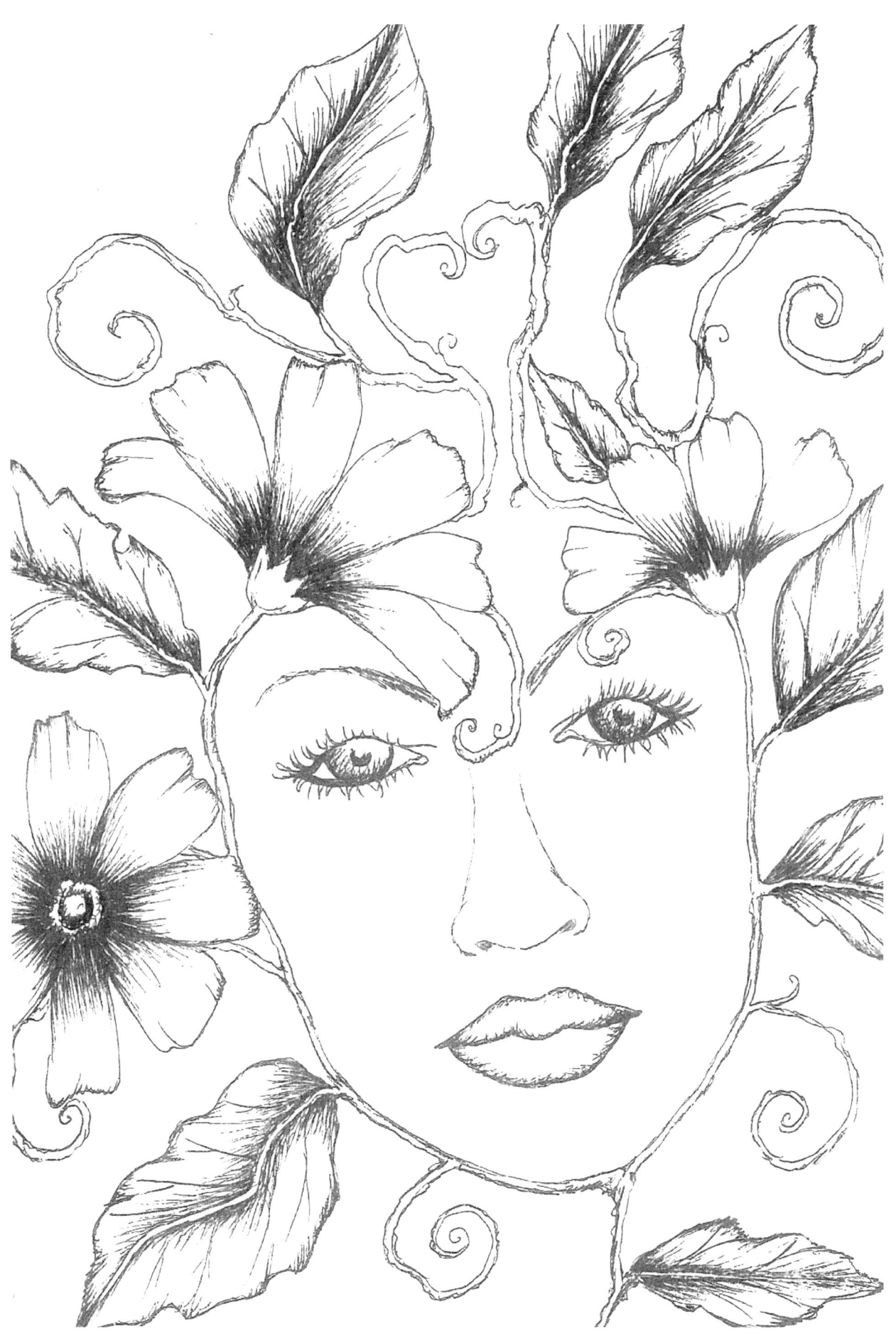

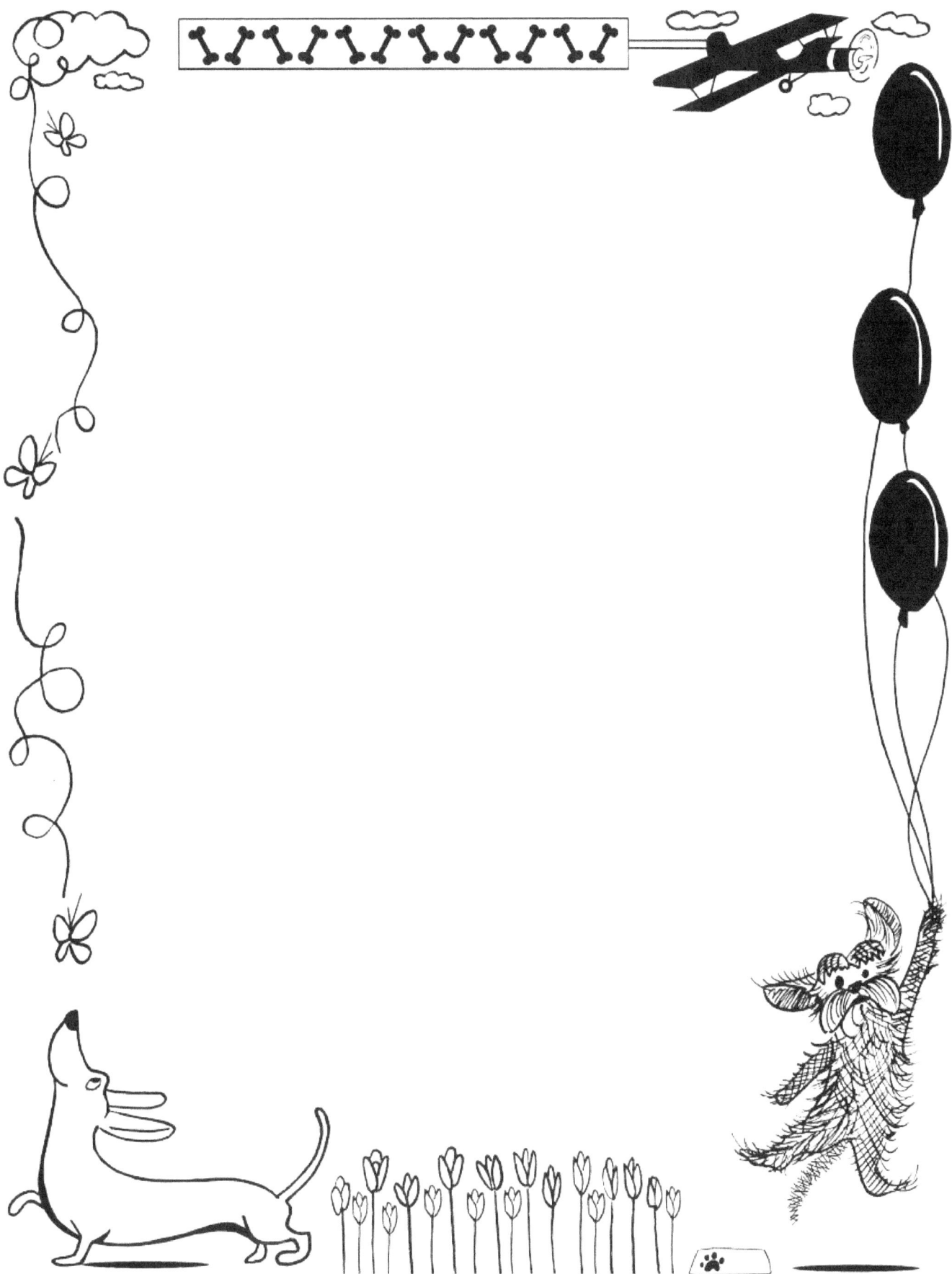

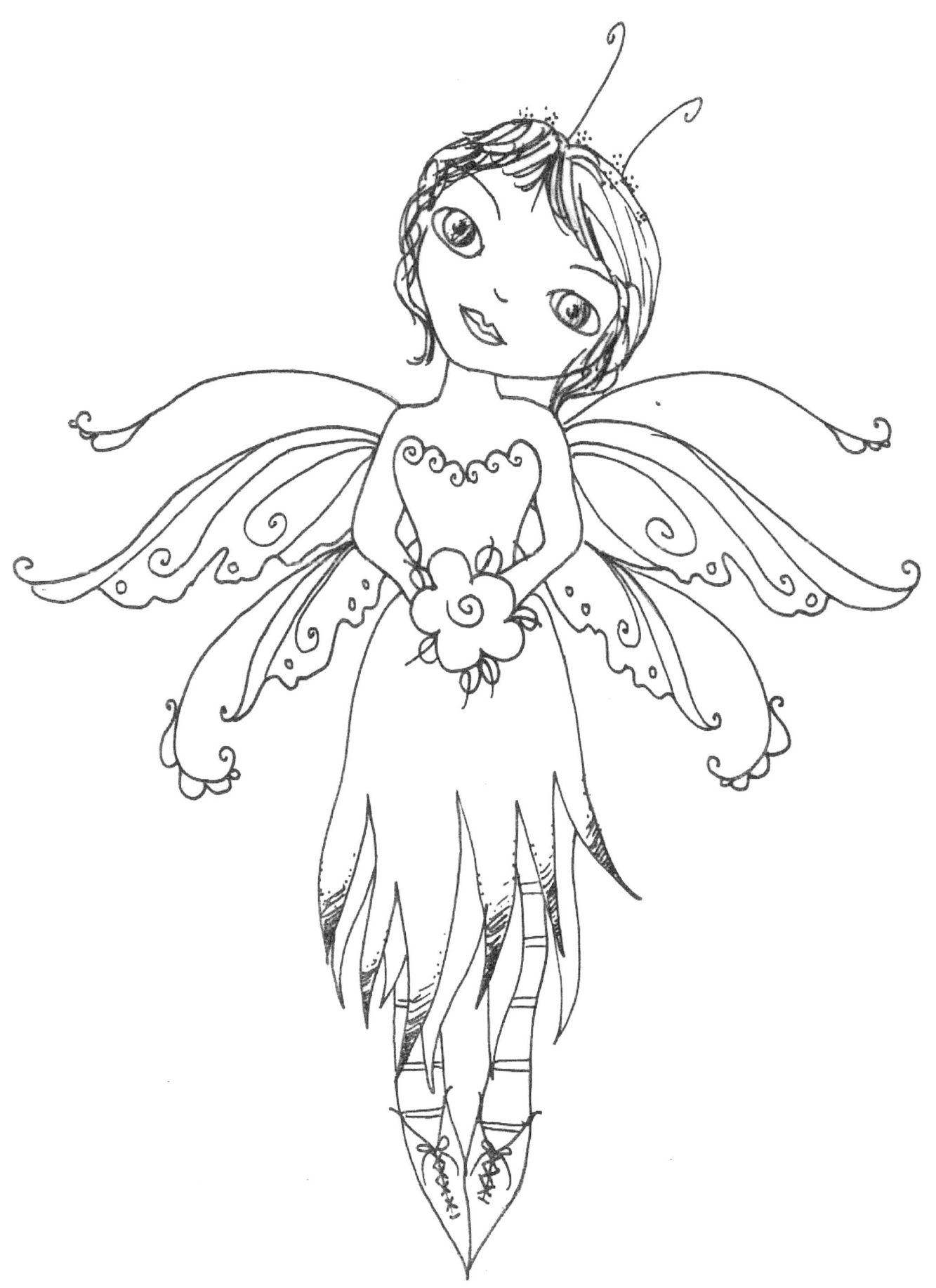

MANY THANKS TO THE FOLLOWING TALENTED ARTISTS:

1. EMMA MAY
2. ANNIE CLEMENS
3. MARIA FERNANDA LEMA
4. HAUER GLASS
5. ANLI ENGELBRECHT
6. LYNNETTE BRITT
7. PAWSOFLOVE PRINTABLES
8. JEAN JEPPSON CLAY
9. SONIA FROM DIGITALARTEM

KEEP COLORING IN THE NEXT VOLUME

OF OUR UNIQUE COLORING BOOKS SERIES!

THE MOTHER AND DAUGHTER TEAM